DANDELION
—— *of that* ——
WINTER

An Autobiography by
Jeong Ae Kim Park

Dandelion of that Winter
Copyright © 2024 by Jeong Ae Kim Park
Edited by Cris Storm

All rights reserved. No part of this publication may be reproduced, distributed, or transmitted in any form or by any means, including photocopying, recording, or other electronic or mechanical methods, without the prior written permission of the author, except in the case of brief quotations embodied in critical reviews and certain other non-commercial uses permitted by copyright law.

Tellwell Talent
www.tellwell.ca

ISBN
978-1-77962-375-1 (Paperback)
978-1-77962-376-8 (eBook)

김 성 란 목사님

박 정 애 드림

This book is lovingly dedicated to my three wonderful children: Elizabeth, Robert and Andrew.

Table of Contents

Part 1: My Story Unfolds 1
  Spring Awakens from its Slumber... 3
  Here, on this Green Hill... 11
  From Heart-to-Heart... 16
  When the Mountain does not know that it is a
  Mountain... 27

Part 2: My Story Continues... 31
  Vast Open Sea.. 33
  An Ending like a Beginning... 38
  Rustle, Rustle Shattered Glass... 43
  A Being without Being... 48
  Calm Courage... 53
  Pat, Pat... 58
  The Strength to End Things 64
  A Stone Hidden in the Mist 71
  Looking up at the Sky in the Fog... 80
  Shattered... 87

Part 3: My Story Lasts Within Me................................... 99
  Gathering Life... 101
  A Farewell Hard to Shake Off... 108
  Hard Goodbyes... 112
  After Crying for a While 115
  Missing Myself... 124

Here, Again, With a Blooming Heart… 140
Relying On My Self…...145

Part 4: My Story Approaches its Closing....................................151
Not A Recollection, But A Memory… 153
Strong Yearning… 165
Even Though I Forget and Moved On… 172
Giving Myself to the Arms of The World… 176

Part 5: My Story Concludes for Now..181
The People Who Made Me Who I Am… 183
The Time It Took to Make Me… 192
Love Confession…Love is Okay. 197
Testimonials… 203

About the Author...215

Dear Reader,

There are many fears and concerns about writing this book. My memories of the past are vivid and releasing this book makes me feel exposed.

It has been over fifty years since I began writing about my life. I was unsure if it was pride or embarrassment, yet this inexplainable feeling tied me down and allowed me to write about my day-to-day life in hiding. I was hiding from an enemy, but not the kind you are thinking about. The enemy was someone near and dear to me. They were from my own culture, from my own family.

I set off looking for more learning opportunities and ended up settling in an unfamiliar land, wishing for a cozy family life, and it has now been over thirty years since I divorced. I never dreamt my life would turn out this way. Not in my wildest dreams did I see myself divorced in a new and foreign land.

I kept silent about my experiences and family affairs and buried these sentiments deep within me. I did not realize at first that it would bring more misunderstanding and pain, making it difficult to fix my mistakes. But this is the norm in my culture and partly, it is also due to my reserved nature.

My children, especially my daughter, witnessed my life up close and encouraged me to write about the past. She insisted the writing exercise would be therapeutic. But thinking of my past always made it difficult for me to breathe and made my chest heavy. Fifty years went by just like that- writing and stopping repeatedly. I had so much to say, yet the words did not always flow like a river into my pen.

Finally, I decided to stand up for myself at seventy-seven to resolve the knot within my heart and reflect on my memories without blaming anyone, including myself. Once I started writing, I could see myself and the path of my life vividly in my head. The journey I was on became clear once I faced my fears and my own ego. I was finally able to find my true self and put my life on paper.

During my reflections, I asked myself a question: 'What am I living for?' I wondered why I could not find the courage to take off the mask I was wearing and why I did not choose a different path. But I think everyone goes through this uncertainty. Everyone asks themselves, "What if?," at least, I think they do. I criticized and comforted myself by asking these questions and eventually finding peace. I learned about who I was by overcoming my regret and pain. I learned that whenever anyone comes to that metaphoric fork in the road, they must choose whether to go left or right. No one can predict their outcome. You just have to accept the decision you made and go on from there. Once I accepted this, I understood the father of my children and the people that played pivotal roles in my life.

Reflecting on my past and the people around me with a more enlightened point of view freed me from the unnecessary feelings I had felt for a while.

I also realized that if I focused my mind and ground it with strong faith, I could overcome any prejudice I might experience from society. I learned that the strength to free myself from other's opinions lay deep within me. Writing while reflecting on my past experiences gave me these precious revelations.

Now, I feel I have achieved inner peace and freedom. I am unsure whether I achieved acceptance but that is not important to me. The thoughts of others do not bother me anymore. The only homework I have left with for the rest of my life is helping others and being generous to make my life more bountiful and joyous. Although I began writing to show my children that I am now free from the burden of the past and I am at peace, I hoped this book could help single parents who have experienced mental and physical domestic abuse and kept it to themselves and suffered in silence.

Thank you, Soon Mi Jung, who helped make this book come true. My sincerest gratitude also goes out to Jamie Park who helped me translate the book from Korean to English. As well, my heartfelt appreciation goes out to Cris Storm for editing my manuscript and helping me through the publication process.

The most precious treasures I have left with me are my children, who have validated my existence as a mother for the past fifty years, and my friends, family, and the organizations that have helped and supported me.

You are all the light of my life.

Sincerely,

Jeong Ae (Kim) Park.

PART 1

My Story Unfolds

Spring Awakens from its Slumber...

The harsh winter days that seemed so endless were finally fading away. Everyone had endured the pain of another cold, bitter season, and no one realized spring had come around. It arrived slowly and creeped into our lives without notice. But before anyone could celebrate the end of winter, we had to go through a painful ritual where we waited at death's door and held our breath for a new awakening and rebirth. My town typically endured a cruel and war-like winter, and we barely held on to our tethered bodies and minds all the while unsure if the bitter cold would ever leave. It was a time when people struggled to perform the most basic survival tasks each day. In these times of uncertainty, words like *dream* and *hope* felt fictitious. Nonetheless, those words alone were enough to get through those jarring winters and sour existence.

Just ten years after the liberation from Japanese colonization and the tragic war of fratricide, I began the start of my twenties. This should have been a time when a young woman would have the freedom to find herself, sharpen her identity and chase her dreams or run wild like a majestic mare in pursuit of her strong stallion. But my young adulthood was precisely at a time when our nation was in recovery. I did not have the opportunity to live a carefree life and follow my wishes and desires. I had to be practical and responsible.

The survivors of the Japanese colonization were akin to wild grass. They pierced the frozen ground all winter, although they remained close to the surface to avoid the frigid, aching wind. They chased a single ray of warmth and broke through the frozen ground; however, to prevent resurfacing to the icy air hovering just above, they needed to crouch close to the ground, looking for the warmth they left behind in order to survive. That was the life of wild grass.

People still found comfort in cliché sayings like *'after every winter comes spring.'* But everyone had some trauma buried in their heart, planted with a very tiny seed of hope. They were anticipating the spring that would come one day and dreamed of the flourishing greenery and vibrant colours that would serve to alleviate the dreaded trauma left in their souls.

From 1960 to 1970, Korea underwent rapid change. The country was left to pick up the pieces in a war-torn land and the people poured their efforts into this communal renewal, whether voluntarily or through coercion. This resulted in unprecedented growth on a global level.

All types of political and social corruption were accepted under the blanket term of *modernization* and *growth* while ignoring the human rights of the people. It was a time of poverty and pain, yet no one doubted that good days would come one day. The positivity that prevailed was hope that allowed people to carry on enduring their pain.

It was an era when everyone lived daily with the hope that the sweat of today's hardships would become sweet rain to moisten the soil, sprout seeds and bear fruit tomorrow. The populace believed that the shabby appearance of the country was just part of a process when we would all wake up to a beautiful and bright future.

I was born in Incheon, South Korea. It is a port city just bordering the capital of Seoul. I grew up there through the liberation. The circumstance of war took my father away when I was five years old, and we had to uproot to Gwangju, where my mother's relatives lived since we no longer had a patriarch to provide for our needs. I wish I could reminisce about my father and recall his face, his voice, his smell but most, if not all, memories I had of him relied heavily on the stories the rest of my family told.

A friend of my father visited one day, although I did not remember him, I could tell by his longing face that he had many anecdotes to share. After seeing me, he said, "*You must be Ggwongja.*" I didn't know how to respond. Was he referring to me? Was this a nickname my father had given me? The man who endlessly called me Ggwongja told me that my father often hunted pheasants when my mother was carrying me in her womb and that I was fed a lot of pheasant meat. He said I was an exceptionally bright and pretty baby, and this was because of all the Ggwong I had been fed. And just like that, I was in his memory as my father's Ggwongja.[1] Oh, how I cherished this memory that was not mine!

My sister had more memories of my father and often told me I took after him. She said she saw his determination and perseverance in me. He was an affectionate and devoted father, spending most of his time with his two daughters. Those times lingered in my sister's heart and flowed into mine. Cherishing these blossoming memories of our father's love made us miss him even more.

One day, during my childhood, I was sitting in front of the door of my house playing with my older sister when I suddenly heard her utter the words, "*I miss my father.*" I envied my sister for having more memories of my father than I did, but at this moment I felt pity and sorrow for her. It is easier to lose someone you can not remember than to lose someone with whom you have fond reveries. To help her overcome her torment, I told her to look at me, "*You said I look a lot like our father. If you miss him, look at me.*" Many memories have faded, but this memory is still oddly clear. Did my answer comfort my sister or emphasize her yearning for him? At this very moment, I can still feel the warm sun shining

---

[1]   Ggwong refers to pheasant, and Ja is a character commonly found in female names.

upon us that day. My young heart, trying to soothe my sister's longing, must have been basking in the warm sunlight that day.

Even with my father's sudden absence, our mother was able to raise all four of us with the help of our grandparents, who were financially comfortable. Thanks to our mother, who studied classical Chinese and calligraphy, we did not have to struggle as much as others to make a living. In addition, my family's unique belief that education was not an option, but a necessity resulted in many learning opportunities for all four siblings. This upbringing conditioned me to believe that learning is not a choice but a part of everyday life that must be experienced.

Although I was financially better off than others, my father's absence left me with a void that could never be filled. On days that I went over to friends who were more prosperous than our family, missing my father would lead me to grumble beneath my breath. In the eyes of an innocent child, any household with a father lived better than anyone else and was more respected in the community. In my naïve mind, any other family with a father seemed happier I thought. My sentiments were resentful, "*Why don't we have a dad? Why don't we have more money?*," I asked my mother. She simply responded, "*I wonder why.*"

I recall my mother letting out a small sigh along with those words, holding back a look of irritation. Back then, my mother often unapologetically expressed her thoughts on how much of a fight and struggle it was to make a living as a single woman. Thinking back, she was justified in her frustration but how could I possibly empathize with her?

Sixty years felt incredibly long then, and I naively thought most people's life span was around sixty years. I mischievously thought that if my mother could not reach sixty years of age, I wished God would give me the remaining time so I could live longer. Looking back, I cannot stop laughing at such a childish and insincere thought. To this day, there is no way I can fathom the loss and despair that my sweet mother faced, having to bury her bright young husband and leaving her alone and forsaken with all of life's hardships. Those hardships were written all over her face with fine lines that clearly spoke volumes.

During the Joseon[2] period, Japanese imperialism overtook the country after a prolonged period of feudal governance. Young intellectuals of that era felt a need to show compassion and take responsibility for the suffering and starving populace. The people toiled all day without respite, and their labour was compensated with a mere pittance of barley. Living in a country that had lost its sovereignty was our reality and, dreaming of a country where everyone eats and lives well, was an elusive and precarious thought.

Capitalism and communism both felt very new back then. No one could debate the differences between ideologies in a suave and sophisticated way, nor could they close in on the differences. It was difficult to understand these novice doctrines that were so unfamiliar to us all, after being accustomed to Japan's occupation and oppression of our people. It was a time when there was no political power to help us understand and come to terms with these differences after the establishment of Japan's violent rule throughout our land for years. It was also a time when violence was the only way to rule over these political distinctions. When one does not understand something, one tends to either ignore it or fear it or rebel against it. In the end, even the most aggressive and terrorizing of all wars could not dissolve the differences of our people, and to this day, we must live with the pain of separation of our country.

My father was a middle-class intellectual who had never experienced hunger; sharing food with the starving neighbours was probably his way of maintaining his humanity and duty. He must have dreamed of a country where minimum fulfilment was always met at the least, even if you did not receive abundant compensation for your work. He would not dare imagine a

---

[2] The Joseon Dynasty lasted from 1392 to 1910 and is the last kingdom Korea which lasted over 500 years and faced invasions from Japan and China.

situation where his way of thinking became the reason for killing and dividing the country in half. That was a tragedy that no one could predict. But his compassion was shown when he would share stacks of rice bags in our yard with people who would not survive the chaos of the Korean War, and he eventually also died in that same fight. Father's absence lasted long within us, leaving despair, poverty, and grief.

My mother could not express her sorrow for her beloved husband in front of others. It was not the way of our culture. Expression of feelings was not seen as honourable but rather, a weakness. She had to remain stoic at all costs. She had four children, so she could not end her life even if she wanted. It did not take long for me to notice that time had stopped for her after my father's death. For me, life was still overflowing with curiosities and things I wanted to do. Life was worth living.

As a child, I had a lot of curiosity and wonder about the world. I strongly desired to jump into the world and experience many new things life had to offer. Being a girl and not being rich enough were not massive barriers for me. I always focused on what was possible and how it was attainable in my given situation. This positive attitude was innate in me and helped me trudge on even in the harshest of times.

I tried my best to achieve everything I could in any given situation. I was active with an unusual driving force and became the student council leader, directing my passion toward participating in many different parts of the school organization. Balancing opinions and participating in healthy debates with colleagues excited me; every moment was enjoyable. The happiness I experienced working with others and learning to work for others rather than just myself was the time when I discovered the joy of giving.

I wanted to study in Seoul to see the bigger world, but I still needed to recognize our financial situation. It would not be easy moving to the big city given my economic state. My grandmother advised me to go to teacher's college and get a stable job to help my single mother. Back then, there were many technical programs to support the lack of a specialized working force. Especially in education, there was a huge demand for teachers, who were considered part of the professional labour sector. If you went to a teacher's vocational school, which is called teacher's college now, you could teach in elementary school. And if you had a university degree in education, you could teach middle school and high school students.

Low tuition for students and a stable job career in education meant being a teacher was the most reasonable pathway for me to take. Not to mention, it was also my grandmother's advice which I could not ignore. I could not be stubborn about my wishes. I had to do what was expected of me. It was just the way it was, like it or not.

I am unsure if it was my trust in my gut intuition or my positive attitude, I somehow always had certainty about my future. Deep inside, I had the confidence that I could do anything. I believed that if I focused and worked hard, I could attend university and study abroad. Those beliefs and my positive thoughts were asleep within me that spring. My winter, still dormant in me would soon wake up in spring, bringing lush greenery and vast fields of harvest to my life.

I received a four-year scholarship from the province of Jeolla, which allowed me to study in Seoul. However, moving to Seoul was not just a matter of paying off school tuition; there were a lot of concerns over a young lady of marrying age living alone in a big city away from her family. Thinking of the excessive cost of living and tuition slowly came to haunt me.

To my surprise, a local university, Jo Sun University, offered me a four-year scholarship. But my wishful thinking would not let me give in to my reality. I wanted to go to Seoul even if it cost too much. I was yearning to live on my own in the big, powerful city. I thought I needed to go there to succeed. Still, the general secretary, Jo A-Ra of YWCA, who was a dear friend and mentor, advised me to approach my situation more realistically and pragmatically.

The general secretary, who always cared for and looked after me like a mother, gave me her opinions on whether it would be feasible for me to balance work and school in an unfamiliar place without knowing a single person. Her philosophical question, *"Why are you trying to be the tail of a cow when you can be the head of a chicken?"* swayed me. I realized that what and how I was studying was more important than where I was studying. And just like that, I accepted the four-year scholarship and attended the local university's biology program. After graduating, I continued supporting the local YWCA out of gratitude for the general secretary's endearing advice. I participated in communal tasks for the betterment of our local community. I put my all into the work that I was doing and put my best efforts into everything I did.

Here, on this Green Hill...

Focusing on modernization and industrialization after the war, South Korea needed a strong labour force in every part of society. They did not hesitate to utilize foreign aid to sponsor young individuals with immense potential and send them to study abroad.

Universities created more diverse programs to cultivate a more significant and specialized labour force and encouraged young adults to attend. The political agendas were set when the country's policies and infrastructure were not yet stabilized, leading to regional disparities and development imbalances amongst cities. The provincial universities were less adequate in areas like operations or infrastructure compared to their more urban counterparts.

After considering many perspectives and concluding that it all depended on how successful I was in my program, not how prominent the program was compared to others, I decided to attend the least financially burdening school. Choosing a university to attend based on this reason alone was far from the learning environment I had expected. Initially, I struggled to adjust and often thought of transferring to a school in Seoul while I went hiking every week. As I climbed through the rough terrain, I wondered why my life had to be so convoluted.

During winter break, my friends and I loaded a handcart with coal and delivered it to local homes. The money earned from delivering the coal was donated to the orphanage we often visited. I wanted to experience and learn from those who were less fortunate than me. The learning moments I found at the university while being around people in a more impoverished situation than I was in resulted in life lessons that could never be taught even by the most qualified professors. Because of these volunteer experiences, university life became fun and busy with various events in which to participate.

I always had a lot of friends around me. Men and women gathered to study and discuss various subjects, which was a new experience for me. With innate sociability and an open mind to unique learning moments and experiences, I began to participate in school and the local communities actively. Along with other youth of that time, I faced the trauma of our time and the absurdity of our society and yet, I slowly developed into a healthy community member.

Despite my progressive mindset and enrollment in a modern school system, conservative Confucian beliefs still influenced my psyche. These norms had become ingrained in me, controlling my thoughts and actions without realizing it. Even my highly educated mother subscribed to patriarchal Confucianism, instilling ethical values favouring male dominance over women. I did not give much thought to women's rights or values then.

Our clothes changed from the traditional hanbok dress to Western attire, but even in the middle of summer, our clothes were buttoned to the very top. Even if no one told me to, I was careful with my posture and kept a physical distance from the male students. Women who tried to leave that framework were criticized for not being chaste, so I subscribed to this influence to avoid criticism from my peers. Fortunately, we had it better than the generation before, but we were afraid to seem ungrateful, so we could not stand up to injustice and irrationality towards women. Perhaps we were even scared of being labelled as 'aggressive women.'

In any era, waves of change are followed by positive and negative second waves. The waves of change I faced in my twenties came like a storm and enriched my life, but the country's foundation was not prepared enough to bear the sudden surge of change.

In those days when we were busy adapting to the immediate changes, our generation could not predict the injustice that the irrational binary moral concept would bring. It was challenging to understand what was societally accepted, and even if we became aware of it, we were too weak to fight against it vocally. Despite that, I had allowed myself to be thankful for what I had rather than be upset about what I did not have. This led me to accept life with an open heart. Although clumsy and inexperienced, my heart was youthful, and my gaze towards the world was sometimes seen through rose-coloured glasses.

I was always understanding towards the world and the people around me. There was always something to do in the world and leave my mark. Deciding what to do with whom and how became a part of my everyday life and my purpose for learning. I wanted to have a positive impact. I joined multiple organizations to give a helping hand to various community issues and actively participated in YWCA's community programs, where my aunt worked as a director. I enjoyed doing something for others and was happy to socialize and express my thoughts. I was excited to volunteer and enjoyed living in harmony with others. Most importantly, I was thankful for being able to share my kindred talents and whatever material possessions I had with those in need.

Volunteering as a teacher at the literacy class operated by the YWCA was also a significant learning period for me. I spent time with those unable to complete their education for various reasons. I appreciated the joy of sharing my knowledge and resources with others. I am grateful for these experiences as they taught me that the more you share, the greater the joy you feel. As time passed, I witnessed students benefiting from this approach. I would see my students passing their General Education Development (GED) test and attending prestigious universities, and it filled me with indescribable pride and happiness. I taught them my knowledge and learned from them the meaning of life and the goodness and joy that comes with it. The learning space I shared with them was like another school to me, and our time together provided valuable learning opportunities and unforgettable experiences.

When I started university, I joined the Hung Sa Dan Academy, also known as the Young Korean Academy. I greatly admired Ahn Chang-ho's teachings and philosophy and was thrilled to participate in various activities he facilitated. His words, "A stone pear grows on a stone pear tree, and an acorn grows on an acorn tree," inspired me to believe that we receive what we strive for. His teachings also helped me develop a solid moral compass, which guides me on how I live my life today. I attended seminars with speakers from all over the world and learned vicariously from their experiences. I pledged to always live with dignity and uphold the academy's values, never to disgrace it.

I strongly believe in the beneficial impact of education and its ability to assist the world for the better. Acquiring knowledge is not only valuable, but it is also a delightful activity, in my opinion, especially when done collaboratively. This belief has motivated me to continue learning and expanding my knowledge. However, I did not stop at merely learning; I began contemplating how to share this knowledge with others. The feeling I experienced when my knowledge was beneficial to others was uplifting, and I am grateful for having such a remarkable experience.

During my time in Korea, numerous political issues needed to be addressed, and I actively participated in raising awareness about them. It was a time when people prioritized efficiency and productivity over human rights and environmental preservation. As a result, I felt a profound sense of concern and responsibility for my society. Although I had limited means, I shared what I had with others and sought to learn from them. Rather than criticizing those who did not share and help others, I started by sharing the small things I had and offering my time to volunteer in various organizations. This approach has allowed me to continue socializing and connecting with others to this day. Perhaps I failed in changing the political and societal notions in Korea at the time, but I assembled small building blocks made of good deeds, and this was a mountain made from a small, green hill.

From Heart-to-Heart...

I began my teaching career at a private high school in Jeonju after finishing university. The school was established over a century ago by an American Methodist church and had both middle and high school programs. This school was built in an era when female education was not commonplace but more significantly, it was a part of many historical events such as the 3.1 movement in 1919. Also known as the Sam-il Movement, it was a time when Koreans came together to protest forced assimilation into Japanese culture and called for independence from Imperial Japan. Many years later, in 1960, the school also took part in the 4.19 revolution also known as the April Revolution. Students opposed the oppression by President Syngman Rhee's government, his autocratic rule, electoral fraud and mass corruption. The tall trees surrounding the school were a testament to its rich history and their fresh, leafy scent was a delight to experience.

Students dressed in wine-coloured boleros and flared skirts would stroll around the school, looking like butterflies among the lilacs. In the spring, the scent of lilacs and the students' youthful energy created an atmosphere of hope and passion for the future. My heart expanded and welcomed the world around me. Every moment felt brand new, and every day was filled with excitement. The chance to instruct these young girls filled my heart with confidence and I felt like I could achieve anything. Finally, I felt like my lonely journey had ended, and a joyful and meaningful time awaited me.

DANDELION OF THAT WINTER

My predictions were not wrong. Every day, I learned something new. Teaching these students and learning from them, in turn, I grew more confident in my abilities.

That is where I first met him. Seventy teachers worked at the school made up of the middle and high schools. In an office that thirty-five high school teachers used together, he sat at the desk next to mine. He taught the senior math class in the morning and lectured at a university in the afternoon. He was shy and soft-spoken. He expressed his feelings not with words but by leaving daily drinks or fruit on my desk. Noticing his feelings, the other teachers would tease us by putting our chairs together and telling us to sit side by side. My face would turn red as a tomato, blushing from embarrassment but also from the amorous feelings harboring inside of me.

At the time, he was waiting to be accepted to many different schools in the USA and Canada. Being an international student was only possible for specially selected students. He was known as a gifted person who had never missed first place throughout elementary, middle, high school, and university. He seemed to have an even more promising future as he planned to study abroad. This romantic attraction was new for him and me, who had lived all our lives with our heads buried in books. It was a strange feeling that made our hearts flutter. That is how our love began.

We started to spend more time outside of school and our feelings for each other grew stronger. Our love was so overwhelming that sometimes we acted like little children. When his work ended every day, he would walk me to my home to say good night before he headed to his own home.

"We saw each other this morning at school. Why did you come by again when it's a lot of work?" I would ask him.

He answered, "But that was in the morning, and I missed you terribly."

Some days, he would stay close to midnight and get sad when it was time to leave because of curfew time. The curfew time set by the country restricted people from being out and about from midnight to 4 a.m. back then. If you were caught roaming around during these times, you had to stay at the police station until morning. On days that he stuck around longer, not wanting to leave, he would get caught by the police and remain in the jail cell overnight and go to work wearing the same clothes as the day before without any lunch prepared. That is how deeply he cared for me and wanted to be around me every waking minute.

These sides of him made me feel sure that he adored and loved me. After exchanging shy goodbyes, I would watch as he rode away, and it felt as if all the stars in the night sky were shining only for me. He was an inexperienced scholar who did not know the world, and he was a man who was deeply in love with me.

He was worried about my weak health as I tutored after school, and he said that once we got married, he would let me sit all day and rest. He would gift me expensive presents such as make-up and beautiful clothes. When I had no appetite, he would buy side dishes without his mother knowing and rush over to give them to me, and sometimes he would bring a jug of Deodeok[3].

Through these tender and caring moments, our feelings for each other had grown deeper in our hearts. As if we were playing house, we exchanged our childish love and developed our romantic feelings. I respected his academic knowledge, and his kindness and tenderness lowered my guard. His shy affection felt like he respected me, and my heart opened to his gentle and untiring love.

Because he had to study abroad, he rushed to wed me. Based on social norms back then and my own principles, dating someone meant you would eventually marry them. Melodramatic and theatrical proposals were not customary in those days. So naturally, we began preparing for our wedding as was accustomed after an appropriate period. If the burning and die-hard sensation in us was love, then our love was beyond that. Many women

---

[3] A traditional Korean wine

married when things were just bearable back then, and love started only after you promised the rest of your lives to one another. That is what marriage was like for most people back where I was from. But for me, it was more than that. Marriage was a bond that existed between two people held strongly together by their love and their faith in God. I was also always interested in those who were academic, and his being known as an intelligent scholar allowed me to accept him as a future partner without much difficulty. Of course, I was also physically attracted to his boyish charm and good looks.

The problem with our impending wedding, started from an unexpected place. Once news broke out that I was seeing someone to marry, my mother strongly disapproved. She was worried that he did not have many friends or family because he came from the north and disapproved that he was just a teacher like me. She especially disliked him after meeting him for the first time and noticing his physical appearance. She thought that he looked insecure and not comfortable with his own personality. My mother judged a book by its cover and his cover, according to her, was not right for me.

Although I was in no rush to get married, this disapproval made me feel defiant. I did not understand the reasons for my mother's objections, as she disapproved of his career when I was a teacher myself. Her comments about his impressions felt like fickle complaints. Most importantly, I was worried when he said he would die if he could not marry me. His mother was enraged after hearing the news about my mother's displeasure and asked around to see who I was and what was so great about me that my family would reject her son and push him to his death. I felt like I was wronging him and his mother. My heart was heavy at the thought of bringing heartaches and hardships to the people around me.

When the news of our wedding spread to our teaching community, the older teachers around me were worried that his personality was not the easiest to handle and suggested that

I rethink this wedding. Many of the female teachers gave me unsolicited advice and told me that some men change entirely after marriage. I thought I would be free from these worries and did not overthink them. I thought that my colleagues were siding with my mother, and this enraged me further.

At times, when he displayed abnormal jealousy toward other male teachers, I took it as an expression of love not of a difficult personality. As the objections, references, and discontent towards him grew among the people around me, my defiance grew in turn, and only the reasons to marry him seemed more apparent to me.

Closer to graduating from university, I visited my friend's place. My friend's older sister was about to be married, so she saw a Korean Saju[4] to check on their compatibility as a couple. My friend and I also followed along just for fun. At the time, I was volunteering as a Sunday school teacher. As a devout Christian who attended dawn prayer sessions and Wednesday and Sunday sermons, I did not believe in such superstition. To me, it was all just for entertainment although many people took it seriously.

I followed my friend into the shaman's sacred place, but I quickly became anxious about being there. Worried that God may punish me, I paced in and out of the room, and the shaman suddenly told me to sit down and said,

"You will get married in two years, but you will experience divorce and become a widow."

Noting these words as mere superstition, I dismissed her prediction but worry started to sink into the corner of my heart. Her words created the faintest doubt in my mind, and I wondered if there was any truth to her forecast and if I was destined for an unhappy life as others had warned me.

I prayed after coming back home. Dreaming of a future where I can walk home with my husband and children on a brisk and sunny morning after attending an early religious ceremony, I begged God to grant me this gracious wish. While preparing for

---

4   A traditional Korean fortune teller

the wedding, if I heard anyone's worried sigh, the shaman's words would resurface and bring me distress. I started to wish I had never gone to see the shaman and realized I made a grave mistake because that visit that was supposed to be for fun turned out to give me a lot of unnecessary stress before our nuptials.

After overcoming several mountains of worry, we decided to have a small, modest wedding. Instead of sending out invitations, we sent postcards to our friends, colleagues, and family to inform them of our marriage. He was popular among the students for being a young and competent teacher; some students even had crushes on him. I would often hear the cheerful laughter of students in his class, even though it was a challenging math class. I knew many of these students might attend our wedding to get one final glimpse of their beloved, unattached teacher before he was no longer single and available.

As our wedding approached, I received a call from the mother of one of my students asking me if I really must marry and explained her daughter's overwhelming heartbreak. Although I was taken aback, I knew she was not the only student with a crush on my fiancé. I decided to let it go and accept the situation as a young schoolgirl crush on her teacher. To avoid any impulsiveness from heartbroken teenage girls, we married in Iri (now Iksan) with close relatives, friends, and a few colleagues present.

Only two of my closest friends attended our wedding. Okran was my best friend throughout middle and high school, and we continued to stay in touch while she juggled work and school simultaneously. Eventually, she went on to get her Doctorate and became a professor of literary studies. She helped me get into my second-hand wedding dress, but Okran touched up the details to make it look prettier, saying, "You will only wear this dress once."

With blessings and congratulations from those around us, we humbly headed to our honeymoon in Onyang. It was a spa town in the middle of South Korea with many outdoor hot springs and indoor hot water baths, both of which had therapeutic effects. After arriving at our accommodation, we learned that honeymooners could bathe together in the hot spring, something I would have never dreamed of or done willingly. I remembered my twelfth-grade teacher's words, "Women must not show their naked bodies even to their husbands. By covering your naked body, you can be respected as a mystical and wise wife." These words were engrained deep in my mind, so I decided against bathing together.

The hot spring water looked warm and comforting, and I could not wait to step in to the sanctity of the warm water and relax my body. While getting ready to wash up, I heard a knock on the door. He took off his socks, and said, 'Wash this,' and threw them at me as if speaking to his subordinate. I was left shocked and confused. I did not understand what happened, and I tried my best to figure things out while being stunned by his action.

He had never spoken to me without honorifics or used coarse words at me. Just a few hours ago, he talked to me with the upmost respect and called me Ms. Park. I thought, what happened? Had I done something to offend him? Is this how marriage is? Is this what my friends meant when they said marriage changes a man? The cold thought slowly crept into my heart. I did not feel this type of chill even when a fellow teacher who married around the same time as I explained to me her thoughts about the reality of marriage. She married after ten years of courtship. About a month into their marriage, Ms. J, who was the Language teacher, missed work which was out of character for her. To check on her out of worry, I visited her home. She opened the door with bruises on her face and neck and invited me in. "My husband and I were not married, but we were together for ten years- practically family, and now I have learned more about him in the past month than in the last ten years." And she showed a weak smile. I did not understand what she meant then, but I suddenly remembered her haunting words. 'Is marriage about men and women being together as equals or is it really a policy that allows men to feel like they own women?' I thought. We both signed our marriage certificate, did we not? We both expressed our vows for better or for worse, did we not? Oh! But I promised to obey, did I not? Then, it was my fault for not seeing the true intention of marriage. I agreed to this one-sided policy. I felt swindled and deceived! Even though I sensed an uneasiness about this arrangement, I did not let it bother me for too long.

After spending the night with my now husband, we officially became married. I gave him all of myself with love and trust, and I accepted him. Exhaustion and nervousness tired both my mind and body. We were now a lawful married couple tied by faith and affection. While I was lying silently with this thought, he said the unexpected. According to his seniors, when you spend your first night with your wife, her hymen rips and bleeds, and she will feel pain. He declared I was not a virgin since I did not bleed or express pain. Since he was a virgin and without much worldly experience, he must have believed such illogical and scientifically false theories. Unfounded suspicions took place in his heart just like that.

A woman's intimate area is biologically just part of her reproductive system, but for centuries, her sexual organ was used to prove her virtue. Doctors can not always explain why this thin barrier sometimes ruptures or at times stays intact. It can be broken by doing the most basic exercises, and sometimes, it can still be found unharmed after childbirth. The power that the hymen had in symbolizing female virtue and to determine a woman's pureness was widespread. In the old days of monarchies, a woman's virginity was determined by the blood of a parrot. One would drop a parrot's blood on their arm, and if it stayed, they were a virgin; if it dribbled off, they were not chaste. In contrast, the hymen is slightly more scientific than a parrot's blood, but I can not think about these audacities without feigning a smile.

People were putting complete trust in such unscientific methods to determine a woman's purity, while no attempts were made to determine a man's virginity. A person's virginity status was used as a weapon and without realizing it, my husband and I became victims of this distorted concept of purity. We faced a sad reality where we hindered our happiness and dignity because of these false pretenses.

I had no reason to feel guilt or shame as I did not take his suspicions seriously. God and I both knew of my chaste heart and body. I did not think anyone, least of all my husband, would doubt this truth. How could he listen to such nonsense and question me? These thoughts upset me, and I did not know I needed to resolve this doubt rooted deep in his heart. I was offended by his impression of me and for him to have such suspicions. It quickly appeared to me that we had different ideas and beliefs, and we slowly began to enclose ourselves in our own schemes.

The next day, we exited the motel that faced a small mountain and took a walk. Leaves hinted at the early summer freshness, and birds flew high with cheerful songs. It was as if mother nature herself was blessing my future. I walked silently beside him as he ripped apart a leaf piece by piece, and I did not know why he became a stranger overnight. I worried he had something uncomfortable he could not share, and I felt impatient.

"Are you feeling unwell?" I asked.

To my question, he answered curtly, "I'm fine."

"Then what is it?" I asked again.

"I said I'm fine," he replied with irritation.

We cared for each other so much until this moment, and seeing this sudden change in tone and action left me stunned. What use was it swearing to live well together before others and God? Seeing him treat me as his object to control and manhandle made me question if he used the marriage practice to own and dominate women.

"Let's go down. As soon as possible." I said to him, as being there, in our honeymoon paradise, had no purpose anymore.

In the field and on the train back home, we became strangers.

That marked the end of our honeymoon, and then we started to head back home to Jeonju. Most women had to quit work after getting married back then. I, too, had accepted a clause when I first got hired that stated I needed to resign after getting married.

DANDELION OF THAT WINTER

Despite that, I was able to stay at school even after I wed. Around that time, our students in the senior class finished their national university entrance exams. Students expressed that the biology exam was the most manageable thanks to me for preparing them well, which made the principal proud of my abilities and so kept me on staff despite my martial status. Furthermore, when I was selected as a Jeonbuk representative to participate in the Jeollabuk-do Biology Teacher Training Institute at the national competition held in Seoul, the principal's confidence in my ability increased, making it possible for me to continue working.

After returning from our honeymoon, we visited his grandmother, who lived in the countryside, as she could not attend the wedding due to her advanced age. Dinner time arrived, and steamed chicken was served. Grandmother-in-law deboned the cooked chicken and ate it at the table with him, even placing the meat of the chicken on his spoon. Grandmother treated him with exceptional care. My mother-in-law and I ate with our plates on the ground, eating the broth and only a few pieces of meat that grandmother gave us. My sister-in-law could not enter the room and had to eat in the hallway with only a spoon. They said girls could not use chopsticks and had to use spoons only.

The division between men and women was strict, and in many areas, men's status and the way they were valued were higher than that of women societally. Dinner customs seen at his home were beyond my imagination. They were discriminating with food, location, and even utensils. I felt uncomfortable that gender created such a great division in his household. After dinner, he used his grandmother's lap as a pillow and read books while his grandmother was chasing away bugs from his head while he read. It was a moment that made me question my husband's views of a women's value and identity. It became evident to me that he was raised with morals and ideals that favoured the male species. This was hard for me to accept.

Just like that, a strange married life began. Sometime later, he received acceptance letters from six different universities across the United States and Canada. He had never missed first place all throughout his education, so those around him congratulated him and said it was to be expected. Compared to the United States, Canada had better social security and considering the scholarship offered, he picked Windsor University in Canada. Once his destination was decided, things got busy preparing for his absence. I was frantic from adjusting to my new role as a wife and daughter-in-law while balancing my work at the school. There were three months left before his departure. That is how we started our new life as husband and wife: A swift hello followed by a quick farewell.

When the Mountain does not know that it is a Mountain...

Not long after our honeymoon period, a beautiful life found its way to us. Although our days passed quickly as we were busily involved with all our responsibilities, this sudden news amused and elated us. We were still imperfect at being a married couple, but being parents felt natural and innate.

Excitement almost burst my heart. In his way, he cared for me while I was struggling with morning sickness while working. He brought me things I craved, sneaked away side dishes from his mother, and timidly expressed affection towards me and our baby. It was nothing special but a warm, peaceful, and ordinary time. It was truly a blessing.

One day, after returning from work, I found him sitting at the edge of our porch. Unlike others who may keep their feelings to themselves, he showed off his discomfort and spoke to me as I sat beside him. He said that he was looking through my belongings to pass some time and he came across my diaries from my time as an unwed woman up in the attic. I had been writing journals since I was young and had a vast collection of diaries. Unsure why he was reading my private musings, I looked at him puzzled. He started to kick my legs lightly as I sat next to him. I realized he must have been upset about the diary entry where I talked about when my university friend, P, who had the same last name as me, stole my first kiss while we were on a date.

P was just a friend, and slowly and naturally, over time, we had attempted to go on a couple of dates. Back then, couples with the same last name could not have legitimate marriages and were only accepted as common-law marriages. Children born from these marriages could still get a birth certificate and be listed in the family registry but would have no outside legal protection. Men and women could not be friends in those days. Since it was customary to marry the person you dated, I felt burdened by being his friend. Before we grew to like each other more, I decided to stop seeing P and informed him gently of this resolution. He sat next to me and listened silently, and then he suddenly leaned in and gave me a peck on the lips. I was caught off guard and broke off our friendship immediately. I was offended by his action and could not understand how he could do such a thing, but I also looked back on my actions to remember if I had done anything immoral to lead him on as if to blame myself. P was innocent to the point of naivety and did not know how to express that he wished to continue seeing me and instead resorted to a clumsy kiss to express his feelings. I was even more naïve than him and did not understand his innocent and pure intention. I took his unwarranted kiss as an offence and sent him a letter to break up our friendship. In response to my letter that was filled with displeasure, he wrote, "Rise from a girl to a woman." I was too young to understand what he meant back then, and I could not forgive him for crossing my moral boundaries. After that, I never saw him again and wrote about my upset feelings in my diary.

He kicked my leg again and told me to burn all my diaries. He said I was his first love and accused me of having another lover before him. He did not hesitate to say he came as an immaculate virgin to me while I was "not virtuous." What did he think of me for him to dare say such words about me? These accusations felt unjust and upset me. At the same time, I also thought it may be disconcerting from his point of view. I wanted to give him the benefit of the doubt. But instead, he burned all my diaries against my will, and I was criticized for how immoral my actions were in

DANDELION OF THAT WINTER

the past. From then on, he labelled me as a whore, claiming that I was not pure whenever he would have his outbursts.

Watching my cherished times and memories turn to ash, I questioned again if this was what marriage was supposed to be. I did not really understand what I had done wrong and what I did to deserve this punishment, but he said that he would forgive me just this once. I thought that being married meant women could not preserve and honour their past without their husbands' permission. Regardless of the context or the logical determination of right and wrong, my past was prosecuted under the judge and jury called, "husband." It was disheartening. I can not explain it well, but it was a feeling of hollowness and destitution. I had never felt such emptiness in my entire life.

PART 2

My Story Continues

Vast Open Sea...

Three months later, he headed off to Canada. His hair, cut short like a soldier, departed on a chilly, windy September day. I welcomed and loathed this day at the same time. The only congruence between us was that I would head to Canada after giving birth.

After his departure and before winter came, I laundered and dried his clothes in the sunshine and buried my head in them, tears welling up in my eyes from missing him. I thought that the distance between us would make his heart grow fonder and I daydreamed about the day we would be reunited. Feeling my baby's heartbeat, I had a comforting conversation with my unborn child and reminisced about my longing for the baby's father. As if trying to fill his absence, I worked harder at school and spent busy days preparing for the infant's arrival. I started my day by giving good mornings and playing beautiful music for the baby, and then after school in the evening, I attended knitting class and knitted baby clothes one knot at a time. Every day was filled with happiness and something even beyond that. I relished in the wonder of being a mother and the glory of having a child.

The Visa application process back then was tedious and time-consuming. Not all consulates or embassies were in Seoul like they are today, so documents like biometrics would need to go through third countries like Japan or Hong Kong. Considering this, the time it took to process all the work was unimaginably long and challenging. The length of time it took for my application to be approved was frustrating as I had visions of reuniting with my husband and finally becoming a perfect family.

My husband went to Canada on a Study Permit, and soon after arriving, he started the application for permanent residency. In the 1970s, Canada handed off immigration application papers to international students and encouraged migration. With an application and a letter proving that there is no legal reason for the applicant to return to their home country, permanent residence statuses were granted without a much-complicated process. Not only that, but they would hand out applications to foreigners on the street to encourage immigration. Back then, Canada had a variety of social welfare programs for the less fortunate and new immigrants. Regardless of the Canadian government's generous benefits, we planned on returning to Korea after he finished his schooling. Still, my husband decided to apply for permanent residence so that our family could receive compensation while he was studying. Although I planned to go to Canada with a foreign-student partner visa, I had to start the permanent residence application process unexpectedly. This meant that I had to stay apart from him for even longer after delivery as this was part of the limitations of the application process.

The day my daughter was born was my life's happiest and most gratifying day. Because my husband was not with me, I had prepared a hospital bag and waited for the baby to come at any moment. I remember the day my daughter was born as clear as yesterday. I finished work and felt more tired than usual, so I headed to the public bathhouse for a hot bath. While bathing, I had an odd feeling that only expectant mothers can relate to and headed straight home. My hands immediately instinctively reached for my hospital bag, took a cab, and headed straight to the hospital to deliver the baby. Twelve hours of pain and cramps caused by the violent contractions invaded my body, and I had to endure the excruciating pain alone. After seeing me in much discomfort, the nurse recommended painkillers, but I was worried that it would harm the baby and rejected the analgesic medicine.

For ten months, I did my best not to be sick, and when I was ill, I did not take any pharmaceuticals out of fear of harming the baby. I suffered long hours of aches and pains not to spoil my hard work. When the morning sun began to shine, my daughter came to me with a loud roaring cry. "Your mother has been handling the pain so well; why are you crying so much?" The nurse said, trying to soothe the baby.

Sometime after, I woke up and held my daughter, feeling confused and disappointed. Looking at the shape of my droopy stomach, everyone predicted that I would have a son, so I knit all the baby clothes in blue and white. I dreamed of eating a giant ripe peach one week before delivery, and when others heard of this dream, they said I would have a daughter, but I did not believe them. Because my in-laws were also hoping for a son, I was disappointed that I had a daughter. But soon, all dissatisfactions were forgotten once I held the baby in my arms. Looking at my peaceful and precious baby, I swore repeatedly to be a thoughtful and caring mother. Despite thinking I would be reunited with my husband right away after giving birth, the immigration process took longer than expected, and we had to be apart for two long years.

Although my husband and I were apart, I was experiencing one of the happiest times of my life. The joy that my child brought to my life was beyond my imagination. My husband's daily letters supported me through his absence and brought warm feelings. Letters came every day that even the mail carrier remembered our names. With his letters filled with love and affection, my daughter and I were overflowing with happiness. I spent every day immersed in emotions filled with love as I wrote back to him and even went through the complicated process of sending food overseas, thinking about how difficult it must be for him all by himself. He too, did not shy away from hard work for our daughter and sent us pretty clothes and shoes.

It was a time when my life felt tranquil and serene. Personally, I felt content and satisfied. There was not much I desired except for the day when we could all finally be together. Few people had proper formal wear back then, and when I would dress my daughter in the clothes he sent from overseas, everyone would dote on her with envy. People thought we were lucky to have someone in North America sending us shipments. Unlike today, it was not easy to send packages overseas. We used letter paper made into an envelope using the blue international-only letter paper. There were no computers or phones, but still, we checked on each other's well-being and shared news to share our longing for one another. It is possible that we exchanged more conversations during those two years apart than the rest of our marriage. He usually did not share his feelings and thoughts much, but back then, he sent a letter to us everyday, and I took it to mean that he missed us as much as we missed him. The letters would sometimes arrive late, and to ensure I read his letters in order, he took extra care by labelling them in sequence. How I longed for our infant daughter to meet her father!

I was grateful that my marriage no longer came in the way of my responsibilities at school, and I was recognized for my adept abilities and spent my days busy with work. Even when times were hectic, I was knitting clothes for my daughter, excited to dress her in clothes handmade with love. I worked hard and kept myself occupied, but it was a peaceful time. I did not doubt that at the end of this soothing and harmonious time, greater happiness awaited me. I did not notice the mountain I would need to climb later. And on one relaxing day like any other, the permanent residence approval I had been waiting for finally arrived.

With a resignation letter in my hand, I regrettably visited the school office. Although I knew that once the visa arrived, I would need to resign from the school and go to Canada. I could not help but feel depressed once the day came. Coincidentally, a male French teacher also came by that day to hand in his resignation letter. "Ms. Park, I worked at this school for three years, and this is the first and last time we'll exchange words." He told me that I was never to be found socializing in the staff room and therefore

DANDELION OF THAT WINTER

we did not have an opportunity to get to know each other. After getting married, I kept a safe distance from the male teachers without anyone advising me to. I never had much chance to speak to other male teachers and left the school without exchanging much small talk with other teachers. I responded with a sheepish smile instead.

The school principal said he was sad to see me go. He also graciously offered to employ me again if ever I desired to return and said the school door was always open for me. He thought of me as a capable teacher and would take me back if I changed my mind. Although it was tempting to stay, I put his disappointment behind me and headed to Canada with my daughter clutched in my arms.

The lush green season was ending, and mountains began to be coloured by the fall. Not realizing how tall the hill in front of me was or how difficult it would be to climb; I was in awe of its beauty. My heart was growing bigger with anticipation.

An Ending like a Beginning...

One autumn's day in October, I exchanged goodbyes with my fellow teachers at a bus station and put my best foot forward to Canada with my daughter nestled in my arms. It was a long journey, starting with a train ride towards Gimpo airport and then multiple layovers in different countries and other airports. Still, the hardship of the trip did not concern me as I was excited to reunite our family.

The letters he sent represented his love for us and that took up an entire corner of my suitcase. I set off on this trip wondering what kind of life awaited me in the new and foreign land. Knowing I would return to Korea with him after living and growing together in Canada, parting ways with family and friends did not dishearten me too much. Going abroad was not easy back then and you could not go whenever you wished. So, I was grateful that I had the opportunity to live overseas and learn. Canada was considered a heaven on Earth to Koreans back then due to the well-established social security system.

As if she knew she was about to meet her father, my daughter endured the long flight even through all the transfers. People often say they are both excited and scared when facing a new challenge, just as I was excited and passionate to explore the unknown and learn new things. I left Korea and set foot towards a new chapter in my life. This was a new beginning with a promise of a better tomorrow.

DANDELION OF THAT WINTER

After two years, our little family finally reunited at the Toronto airport in Canada. We did not greet each other extravagantly and express ourselves much, but just smiled at each other modestly, basking in the joy of finally seeing each other in-person. From Toronto, we headed off to Windsor, where he studied. The small and humble city had the charm of an old town. His university had traces of history here and there and it welcomed me. Historical authenticity was found in various parts of the campus but blended well with the youthfulness of juvenile scholars, creating a quaint charm.

He lived in an old rooming house. Most low-income students stayed in this residence. There were many tenants in one small building. It is said that all places where people live are similar, but there was a moment when this unfamiliar landscape felt exotic to me. My fantasy of Western houses seen in movies shattered as I climbed the stairs in the two-storey house. The dusty, squeaky wooden stairs and the house's interior made me think, '*I didn't realize these types of houses existed in Canada.*'

On top of a dirty carpet that looked like it had been there for decades was a round table and a shabby chair. The lumpy bed barely maintained its shape, and you could tell the mattress had sunken from being overused. The windowpanes had paint peeling, looking fragile as if they could break by the slightest wind. I wondered if this was what ghettos were like; the scene in front of me was something I had never experienced before and messed with my mind for a moment. I was unsure if he had to get a place on short notice or if he did not care much about our living conditions because it would only be temporary, but the fatigue overtook my body, and I could not ask the question. Calming my dismay, I tried to channel my positive thoughts and looked around the place once again. '*For now, we are here, but after finishing his studies, we will return home to a better place, so, this is just the beginning, not the end.*' This is what I told myself to give me reassurance. Thinking about why I came to this new land helped me recollect myself. This positive outlook helped me keep my composure when cockroaches or mice visited frequently. Of course, cleaning became my best friend and favourite activity after that.

Since the first week of being together, we were swamped. We were busy unpacking our belongings, which we packed in multiple layers to prevent them from breaking, going around town to say hello to his acquaintances, and getting familiar with new places. There was also a bit of shy awkwardness between us after we were away from each other for two years. Our adorable child would walk around us with her cute tiny stomps and loosen the awkward tension. After settling in a bit more, I had the chance to look around the dwelling and at the corner of my gaze, I stumbled upon a bundle of letters. The joy I felt at that moment thinking that he had kept my letters all this time was quickly replaced with devastation after I learned that the long rolls of letters displayed in the open were not from me.

He was forthright about the bundle of letters after seeing my questioning face. I would have preferred not to hear what he had to say. The correspondences were mostly from different women from around Windsor, writing about dinner dates and meeting up with him. While he was alone, he pretended to be single and met several women for dates. He told me everything openly and honestly as if none of it was a big deal. *'What is he saying to me? Is he talking to me? Does he even know who I am?'*, I thought. The words coming out of his mouth spread heavily around us, but I did not know what he was saying to me. His words were jumbled in my brain and did not make sense. I felt something more than just feeling upset and dumbfounded, it felt like I was absorbed into a numb and insensible world. My atoms were splitting inside of me, and I felt disconnected and lost in the void made by his words.

He talked to me as if he was speaking with a friend, chattering away about how popular he was with women and how many people wanted to introduce him to their daughters or sisters. He acted as if he did not realize I was his wife, or perhaps whether I was his wife was not important to him. He went on to emphasize what a popular and successful man he was. When he told me that another Korean immigrant brought his younger sister, a nurse, to Canada to introduce them and set them up, I felt horror. I was sure that he must not be in his right mind, and he must be sick. The worry whether he was mentally ill swept over me. '*This is not real, it's not my reality,*' I repeated to myself silently. There is no way he is in his right mind, I thought. I believed that the shock of moving to a new country must have stressed him to the point of losing his mind.

Without a single care for my trauma and dismay, he chatted away about a Greek woman he met at the school. He told me nonchalantly that he liked her and wrote a letter to her parents for her hand in marriage, which was rejected. His words were absurd, but I questioned how he could say all these things to his wife and whether I was conversing with a stranger. I started to be afraid of him. All my beliefs, thoughts, and trust in humanity shattered into a million pieces and scattered around me. To this day, I am confused as to what happened to him. Just who exactly was this person, and what kind of flawed character must one have to share those details about infidelity with his wife? Some may argue that it is normal for a married man to have an affair or two or that a man's ability to womanize determines their capability as a man but seeing how easily he could tell lies and carry-out devious tricks made me frightened of him. But more than anything, I was scared as to why he was so willing to tell his wife everything without sparing her feelings, as if it was nothing significant.

Regardless of this inconsiderate and nasty behaviour, I tried to cherish my time with him. The holiness of the promise he and I made under the marriage oath was engraved deep in my heart. I remained loyal to our family and respected him. I had infinite respect for the depth of his knowledge, and his academic achievements were proof of his maturity and humanness. From his letters, I could sincerely feel his consideration and maturity. Was this all a lie and deception? Despair filled my heart as I pictured him with other women. It felt as if everything was over.

Just what was I doing with this person and for what did I come to a new country? Everything felt so unreal. I was losing my sense of reality, and my mind turned blank. I could not think straight, and I could not analyze my situation properly. My life experiences had never prepared me for this kind of traumatic event. I was utterly defenceless as I had never learned how to handle a situation such as this one. In a whirlwind of emotion and confusion, I was in disarray.

My new journey ended before it even started. The hope of this new promised land quickly shattered, and the shards of broken hope stabbed my aching heart.

Rustle, Rustle Shattered Glass...

A few days passed while my senses went numb and my feelings dormant. I was barely holding on if not for my daughter's touch and warmth. It all felt like a bad dream, and I wanted to wake up to a reality where none of this happened. But every time I would wake up, I was in a strange place surrounded by strange events, with him just standing before me acting as if everything was fine. As much as my surroundings became strange and unfamiliar, I felt more unfamiliar with my self. My daughter's face looking back at me was the only familiar face I had there. I hugged my daughter even tighter to avoid being lost in an unfamiliar place and strange world where I knew nothing. Time passed while these unfamiliar feelings swayed me left and right- like being on a boat headed for disaster. But life had to go on if not for my sake, but for the sake of my beloved daughter.

My husband's colleague from the university, H, visited our apartment. My husband was absent, and I was still adjusting to the time difference, so I woke up in pyjamas with messy hair. I opened the door slightly ajar and informed H of my husband's absence. I did not want to show my unkemptness to an unfamiliar man, so I looked through a small gap and said, "My husband is not home right now. Please come back when he is here." I spoke to him respectfully so as not to upset or offend him.

When my husband met H at school, H said, "Your wife is too proud. Women must be beaten every three days to be docile and easier to handle. You have some work ahead of you."

My husband informed me of this discussion with H with a serious expression when he returned from school. I was surprised by the conversations these self-proclaimed intellectuals shared, and the delivery of these words as if to lecture me was even more insulting and unfamiliar.

After a few days, he invited a friend from a different faculty to dinner. After dinner, we shared more conversations, so naturally, our evening extended into the midnight hour. My daughter began to whine as the conversation dragged on. We went into the bedroom, and while I was putting her to bed, I too fell asleep without realizing it. My husband went out to see his friend off and forgot to bring his keys. After he said goodbye to his friend, he could not return to the building because the doors locked automatically from the inside. I woke up to a window breaking and heard him call my name frantically. I rushed down to the entrance and was met with my husband's furious face.

As we were walking up the squeaky stairs, my husband accused me of intentionally locking him out to annoy him, and his anger started escalating.

"You are disrespecting me. You pretended to be asleep." He accused.

"No, I fell asleep for just a bit because I was tired from the jet lag." I explained.

"You. I'm going to kill you tonight. I'll strangle you to death." He threatened.

"Then I will run away, run away and never return." I proclaimed.

I thought he was kidding about his death threat and laughed it off to make him feel better. But as soon as he entered the apartment, he searched for rope. He was unable to control his anger and truly wished to kill me. The explicit violence he was displaying was not fake. It was real. And with that, my heart shattered into tiny pieces and spread across the floor like small pieces of glass, leaving cuts across my body as it lay beneath my feet.

He could not calm down not matter how much I tried to improve his mood. Pointing fingers, yelling, and swearing were not enough to release his rage, and he kept running around the house looking for a rope while screaming,

"Where's the rope?! Rope!"

I watched him behave like a madman as he accused me of intentionally locking him out while running around the house looking for a rope with which to kill me. I honestly thought he was delusional. I was unsure if it was craziness or anger, but I just stood there and watched it all unfold as if my mind had left my body. I became an empty shell. If he succeeded in killing me that night, he would have killed a vacant vessel, not a person with a soul, because my conscious mind had left my body looking for a place to hide.

Finally, a thought already in the corner of my heart crept up as I let out a weak sigh. *'I can't live like this. He has neither faithfulness nor loyalty, and I can't live with a person like this.'* A sigh came from the depths of my heart. Once he calmed down, he justified his actions by saying,

"Women need to be beaten once every three days to behave."

To him, women were less than human. Moreover, he did not consider me as his equal. My heart was breaking. I realized that even with all that education and knowledge, he was a below-average man, and my heart stopped between disappointment and despair.

I remembered the female colleague who mentioned that she learned more about her husband one month after their marriage than during their ten -year dating history. The bruises on her neck and face must have given her deep regret. I also told him before marriage that I could endure anything except violence. I firmly told him we would divorce immediately if he ever became violent toward me. Even while saying that, I did not think it could happen. He did not respond to my words but looked at me straight on as if to challenge me. I realized then how naïve and daring I was. My obliviousness about male domination had led me to blame only myself for being disappointed in my husband's behaviour.

Companionship through love, wholeheartedness, and respect is what I imagined our marriage would be like. I believed we could achieve everything wherever we wanted and overcome anything sincerely without being weighed down by material conditions. For me, the inner qualities of my partner were more critical than anything, and now I was questioning his. Did I mistake his degrees and education as a sign of maturity and sincerity in his character?

I questioned if I had blinded myself with his educational background while claiming not to care for materialistic conditions. My ignorance screamed deep within my heart. The small crack that started in the corner of my heart spread into thousands, millions of cracks and shattered into unidentifiable small pieces that could never be reassembled. Fragments brushed up against each other and ripped my heart into small pieces. It continued to stab my heart and damaged it to the point of no return.

I do not know how I stayed up all night. While sitting in the kitchen chair, I cried and comforted myself while muttering,

"I need to return to Korea. I need to go back home."

My daughter squirmed in my arms, and I could barely calm my heart. She looked at the morning sun that rose without fail and beamed at me like any other day- and it pained me. It hurt me to look at her because I did not know what our future entailed. I was confused. I felt like I was living in someone else's body. This life could not possibly be mine. It felt like an episode of The Twilight Zone.

An unfamiliar woman visited him early that day, and he invited her in as if nothing happened. She had a slender figure and dressed elegantly. She was the nurse invited to Canada to be introduced to my husband. It was Saturday, the day that the local farmer's market was open. They left together to go to the farmer's market to get groceries and soon came back and fussed around the kitchen to make lunch. She glanced at me and then

DANDELION OF THAT WINTER

went to make Sujebi[5] with him. The two prepared lunch together as if our child and I did not exist. This bruised my ego but more than that I felt inadequate in my own home. Did I even have a home? This was not home, was it? Suddenly, I felt out of place and unwanted. If I died at that moment, I would have been grateful for the release from the misery I felt.

I witnessed so much in such a short period, so I thought nothing could surprise me anymore, but it felt like my mind was paralyzed witnessing such deceit. Was the common sense and belief I followed not the norm? It felt as if I was an abnormal person questioning my belief-system. But I was not the abnormal person in this so-called relationship. If anyone was abnormal, it was him. My daughter snuggled closer, and I wanted to cover her eyes and ears to protect her innocence. The sharp glass fragments beneath my feet now felt like spiked shackles holding me back. What will I hold on to so I can walk on this rocky and uneven road? How far have these glass fragments spread? Did I jump into a sea of glass fragments without realizing it? In that painful and vast open sea, I was alone without a visible path. Maybe there never was any road to take. Maybe I had imagined it.

---

[5] Korean style pasta-broth noodle soup

A Being without Being...

I filled out the divorce papers calmly by myself. I gathered all the strength I had left in me and completed the paperwork. I could not feel anger, sadness, or fear; I was just in a state of nothingness and wanted to escape this unbearable situation quietly. Divorce came with lots of obstacles, especially for women back then. Even while knowing this, it felt like divorce was the only choice. It is not like I could end my life, so I should end my relationship with this man instead. I handed him the divorce papers and asked him to return me to Korea. I did not need anything else. I only needed the plane to get to Korea for me and my child. On my way to Canada, I had $80 dollars, and during the layover in Japan, I bought a radio for $60 dollars, so $20 dollars was all I had on me. If I had enough money to buy plane tickets, I would have just left that place with my child, no questions asked. I had a school that would welcome me whenever I came back, and I believed in myself and my abilities, so I did not wish for anything from him. I was happy just returning to the ordinary world I knew.

I informed him of my decision and after an awkward and uncomfortable amount of time had passed, he apologized. He said he went too far this time and was unwilling to divorce, saying that his infidelity was too small of an issue to divorce over. Not a single word of sincerity or admittance of guilt came out of his mouth. His words came from a place that did not truly understand how much he had hurt my daughter and me. He was no expert at expressing his feelings or having a sensitive conversation, so

DANDELION OF THAT WINTER

for him, the empty apologies must have been his best attempt at expressing himself and comforting me.

The apology was not enough for me to let go of everything I had experienced but I could feel the storm in my heart calming. Perhaps I was also looking for an excuse to avoid the harsh road of separation and divorce. So even though it was not enough, and I did not trust him entirely, it was difficult to ignore his apology.

I grew up with the inaccurate societal belief that divorce is not a possibility, and for one to divorce, there must be a detrimental issue on the bride's side. Men are the sky, and women are the ground. Therefore, women were the foundation in a marriage and must endure and be patient with whatever decisions men make; that was the lesson I was taught by my mother growing up. Even if men do something terrible, if a woman could not handle and endure it, it would be the woman's fault back then. It was a time when divorce meant humiliation for a family, and women had to find excuses not to divorce and bring shame to their families. Even if it meant they would be unhappy for the rest of their lives.

I recalled the tearful words of my sister, who was already married. She had a handsome movie star-like husband and experienced countless affairs and domestic abuse.

Worried and upset for her, I asked her, "Why must you live with your husband when you are being treated like that?"

She would look at me with vacant eyes and say, "If I were not the oldest daughter, if I did not have younger siblings who needed to marry, I would not be living like this. I'm scared to ruin your chances of marriage, so I must endure this."

Although my brain understood what she meant, I did not fully comprehend the pain and burden my sister had to carry alone.

Having to endure through moments like this was an absolute humiliation. Above all, knowing the insulting times my family would have to bear with me because of my divorce pained me more than anything. I worried for my daughter's future as a child of divorce. If I just tolerated my husband's behaviour, I would avoid giving my child any insecurities and prevent her from getting hurt by other people's judgements. I became worried that I only cared about myself and did not have concern for my child as much, and I felt remorseful. As I was thinking about my surroundings, it felt like I needed to endure these nonsensical situations. I kept questioning whether divorcing to end this humiliation I was experiencing was worth more than protecting my family and child.

As my thoughts ran on, I wanted to believe that he could change. I tried to justify his unexplainable actions by thinking, *'He must have had his reasons.'* He was so apologetic. It was too unfair of me not to give him another chance, and suddenly, I was blaming myself for his actions and not understanding and enduring it all like a "good wife" should. The thought that 'if I endure everything, then everyone could be happy' kept knocking at my door. *'Yes, maybe he got too lonely from being apart for so long. He'll change back to the man I know. I need to protect this marriage for my child.'* I whispered to myself again and again.

And just like that, I put behind my existence and everything that supported me to live as a meaningful and independent individual.

Some may ask how I could live like that and be okay with being treated so unjustly. I struggled to death to live on. There were too many things that I needed to shoulder, and I tried hard not to suffocate from the weight of these responsibilities. Most importantly, I worried about my family's potential hardships because of my selfish decision. I cared more about my family potentially sharing the consequences of my decision than my own misery.

I felt fear. I did not mind living as a single parent raising my daughter alone since I had a stable job as a teacher to go to, so I did not have any financial concerns. What worried me was the preconceived ideas others would have of me. I did not have the courage to stand up against society's prejudices.

Back then, women were present but did not have a presence. They could only exist within the boundary that society had created for them. Women could only live within the boundaries set by

DANDELION OF THAT WINTER

laws made to benefit men's convenience and were accepted by society as long as they were silent and law-abiding. I knew that I could not live in a society as a person rejected by others. So, I hid my feelings and gave up on separating him.

Today, people, may say that I did not make sense and was making excuses for my weakness. But the fact is that in the autumn of 1971, I lived in a nonsensical time. I was too weak and young to resist or protest. I was just an ordinary mother who cared more about my child's well-being than my own.

The meaning of marriage changed for me; it was no longer a result of beautiful feelings that two individuals shared. It was just a duty one undertook in order to comply with the demands of a patriarchal society. All my vibrant and peaceful feelings made their farewells, and the responsibility of my decision became a challenge that remained in my heart.

In order to exist within the moral standard set by society and to prevent any shame that may fall on my child because of my actions, I decided against leaving him. It was a decision that would require me to give up my independence and my self-respect and it meant that I was also giving up on my true essence. Everything I believed in had to be put on hold for the sake of my daughter. I would need to live the rest of my life pretending not to exist beside him. That was the only way to survive and protect what I cherished. This was a sacrifice I had to make. I was not the only woman in history taking this path. There were other women before me and others after me that did and would do the same for the sake of their family's good name and reputation. This was a path where I needed to abandon myself. It was not courage or bravery but fear that forced me to walk this path. It was a decision that made me give up on myself and deny my soul's existence. But to protect the ones I loved; I was unable to protect myself. To exist, I denied my existence. That was my life. That was a woman's life.

So, I existed without existing. I was always there despite being vacant. You can live on if you have just one thing to hold on to.

No one told me what to hold on to and how to live on, but I just readied myself to sail through the big ocean of shattered glass pieces that glistened like worthless diamonds.

Leaves were yellowing in Windsor when I began to prepare myself for the future. "Soon, there will be snow falling from the sky," I whispered to my daughter, seated on my lap as we gazed out the window. *'I should knit a beautiful sweater for her,'* I thought.

I locked my eyes with her clear gaze, full of innocence. Looking at my daughter's unwavering eyes, I realized that she would be the light I would follow and the purpose of my life no matter where I was or what I was going through. *'Fall is short, and winter will be long, but it's not like spring will never come.'* I thought, reassuringly.

Calm Courage...

Through the aged windows, I observed the daily rise and fall of the sun and learned to appreciate the passage of time. I watched as the colours of the sky and trees signalled the arrival of each new season. Windsor, a border town across the Detroit River facing Michigan state, was fascinating. I was amazed to see numerous Canadians crossing the border day and night to work in Detroit, where the most prominent car manufacturers settled. However, the air quality in Windsor was not excellent, probably due to its proximity to the industrial zone, and the humidity was high since it was close to the five Great Lakes. As a result, the weather was generally sticky and cloudy. But the vibrant community and lifestyle made up for the poor climate.

Living in Windsor was strenuous. We did not know anyone, and I lived alone with my daughter most of the time. I felt as though we were cut off from the rest of the world. My husband had not placed a landline in the house, not wanting me to speak with other Korean women in Windsor. He made excuses saying that they were a bunch of charlatans, and they only wanted to gossip about insignificant matters. He said if I engaged in such practises, it would show inferior manners and feeble etiquette. Eventually, I was left with no opportunities to practice my English. I was so isolated that I even forgot a bit of my mother tongue. Despite this isolation, I still had neighbours in my building who allowed me to feel the warmth and strength of community.

On the floor below us, at a rooming house, lived our old, greying landlady who had previously visited Korea as a missionary and could play Arirang[6] on her old piano. When the loneliness and weariness got the best of me, I would sing along to her piano and weep a little. Sometime after, she offered me the loose sheets of music, asking me to keep them since she did not have much time left to live. I accepted them graciously and held on those sheets of sad musical notes as they were my only few remaining elements of my homeland.

The old landlady was my only window to the Canadian culture since I rarely went outside. One day, I found her preparing to welcome a guest from across the river. She explained that her babysitter, who had watched after her children when they were much younger, was visiting, and she was excited to see her. I was surprised to learn that her babysitter was a black woman. Although I had met many foreigners at the YWCA in Korea, I had never met a black person. I realized that media representations influenced my perspective about black people.

My landlady perceived something in my reaction and told me that she did not care about the colour of her babysitter's skin as long as she could communicate with her, and they could share their food and culture. She was grateful that her babysitter still visited her even after many years. Her attitude and way of thinking amazed me. I realized that I had an unfair prejudice that Asians were better than black people, and it made me reflect on myself and all my preconceived notions I had developed over time. Canada's multiculturalism policy to recognize and coexist with our differences became apparent to me and I realized why it was so important. This policy helped Canada tackle and diffuse any racial or cultural issues that might arise that other countries struggle with, I surmised

Many more opportunities to meet a variety of multi-ethnic people arose after my sudden revelation. Across from our unit,

---

[6] A tragic Korean song about separation and lost love

DANDELION OF THAT WINTER

I had a couple from former Yugoslavia living opposite me. The wife was a beautiful woman with wavy blonde hair and blue eyes, and I thought I would only see such a woman in movies. She had beginner-level English and did not know many people, so she visited me for a chat from time to time. She would often bring bread stuffed with cooked cabbage or bread with various toppings. Later, I discovered that these were called sandwiches and pizza. Since I had never tasted these types of food, it was exciting but not quite to my liking, so I could not eat much of it. Even today, when I see cheese and sauerkraut made of cabbage, it reminds me of her sweet and shy smile. She and I communicated using our limited English and body language to share food and find comfort in each other's loneliness. It helped to pass the time. Although she had no children of her own, she adored my daughter. I wondered if she also missed having her people around her.

As the days passed, I felt I was only living because I was breathing. It was like this involuntary bodily function was keeping me alive and nothing else. My child and I spent countless days stuck at home without the ability to go outside or meet new friends. Nowadays, it is hard to imagine complete isolation when you can easily speak to anyone, anywhere, at any time. But back then, there were no computers, no internet, and even phones were rare, so communicating with family in Korea was a challenge. I would write letters to them in the tiniest handwriting possible, attempting to fit as many words as possible onto the light blue international letter paper. The yearning for social contact was unbearable at times.

A surprise guest knocked on the door as I sat alone, soothing my loneliness with hand-written letters. I was not expecting anyone so I was curious who it could be. When I opened the door, I was shocked to see my middle school homeroom teacher, Mrs. Jeong Sook Ahn, standing there. Her familiar face was like a gift sent from heaven when I needed it most. She explained that she was on holiday in Detroit and decided to pay me a visit on her way back. I was amazed that she had found out where I lived and remembered me after all these years.

When I asked if she remembered me, she replied, "Yes, first-year, room seven, number 7 Park Jeong Ae," while recalling my student number.

Her husband worked as a diplomat at the South Korean embassy in Ottawa, so they lived there together. I was overjoyed to see her again, as her visit was just what I needed to feel like my old self. I felt like I was stranded on a deserted island alone those days and her visit was more than enough to cheer me up and erase the feeling of lonesomeness I had even just for a few hours. I asked her how she found out my address, and she explained that she had asked one of my old homeroom teachers whom I was exchanging letters with regularly.

My middle school teacher's visit brought me some elation, but it was quickly squashed by my husband's adverse disposition towards me. It was surprising to see how patriarchal my husband was. He monitored my every move and criticized everything I did. Even when I cooked dinner, he would complain about my cooking and say that it was like dog food and that he could not eat it. His criticisms never ended, and he would compare me to other wives, which made me feel bad about myself. He said other wives cooked well and looked better and kept cleaner homes. There was nothing I could do right in his estimation.

After finishing university, I went straight into teaching. I always had someone helping me with daily house chores, and I did not have much experience in cooking meals. Notwithstanding, my mother-in-law criticized my inadequate skills and said I was not part of the family. She would even say she wanted her son to marry a woman that was exceptional at housework to my face. I tried my best to match my husband's preferences despite living in a foreign country with limited resources. Still, he never appreciated my efforts or understood my intentions.

Above all, he coerced me to always obey and comply with his wishes no matter what. He repeatedly compared me to dough and told me I only needed to mould to how he kneaded me. Complying to his hierarchical ways was a daily struggle. I had lived as a young professional teaching students back in Korea, and now I was expected to be a dutiful wife, stay-at-home mother and basically a servant for my husband. I was not used to living by these terms and I never anticipated that he would expect me to live this kind of lifestyle. He knew who he had married. He knew I was a young professional with ambitions. If he wanted a handmaid, he should have said so before we got married but he never laid out those conditions.

I felt duped.

Pat, Pat...

Despite being in Canada, which was known to be a paradise on Earth to my people, because of the many assistance programs for lower-income families and free medical care, the cost of living was still a challenge. Back then, $10 dollars could easily feed our family for one week. However, as a student couple who needed to study and work, financial worries were always present. This, of course, added to our burden as a married couple.

Our primary source of income was scholarships from the school. However, my husband struggled to balance school and the bills and oftentimes expressed discontent. It seemed that his dissatisfaction was directed towards me. He would often compare me to other wives and complain about my lack of income. Unlike in Korea, where my job as a teacher was highly valued, it was useless in Canada since I could not fluently speak the English language. On the other hand, nursing was a high-paying profession in Canada. Whenever he found himself in a difficult financial situation, he would reminisce about the nurse he was introduced to after graduating and regretted not marrying her. This comparison humiliated me, and it made me feel worthless. My husband was constantly burdened by financial difficulties, and he constantly expressed his unhappiness about supporting his family. During his youth, he was labelled as a genius and was preoccupied with his studies, so he never prepared for the responsibilities of being a husband and a father. Essentially, the responsibilities of family

DANDELION OF THAT WINTER

life came as a liability to him, and he did not know how to resolve the mental stress that came with it.

To him, even his child was a burden. Because of this, it was hard to expect him to have any fatherly moments with our child. In my mind, I would compare him to other fathers, but I would not dare say any of my thoughts out loud. Other fathers would hug and carry their child on their shoulders, for instance. He did not even lay a finger on her. Our daughter was usually depressed by the cold atmosphere in our household. I felt sorry for her because it was not her fault that she came to be born from a father with no feelings for her. Sometimes, I could feel her shivering when he was around. When I gently stroked her, she would calm down and pat my hands back with her tiny hands. Pat, pat, she would lay her hands on mine rhythmically. A child should not have to console her mother like that or grow up in a miserable household.

Canada was busy with industrialization back then, and the burst in economic growth required many human resources. To satisfy the demands for labour, Prime Minister Trudeau opened the doors to foreign workers and immigrants. The government also made policies to teach new immigrants English to speed up their assimilation. Thanks to the Multicultural Act and these policies, I could also study English. On top of having the opportunity to learn English, they gave students money to help with their living expenses during their study period, and it became my primary source of income. Thanks to that, I could learn English without any financial burdens.

These reasons prevented him from forbidding me to attend English classes. I was finally allowed to go to school and learn English with other immigrants, and I finally had some freedom to breathe. I was so oblivious to Canadian culture after being isolated and finally had the opportunity to go out and meet other people. Oh, how thankful I was for this opportunity. This was indeed a valuable time for me as it helped me improve my English skills and interact with immigrants from different countries by sharing food and dressing in each other's traditional attire to understand one another better. It allowed my daughter and I to appreciate what it truly means to live in a multicultural society and feel one another's warmth and culture.

After improving my English, I visited the Ministry of Labour and Immigration office to seek employment support. I vividly remember how I used my broken English to prove my work ethic and willingness to do any job. My desire to become more independent and stand on my own two feet was insatiable. I wanted to work because to me, this meant more freedom and less time being asphyxiated by my husband's rules.

Through the city's job-finding program, I found a position and started working at a hotel restaurant, making salads. Once summer break started, my husband also started working there in the kitchen. It was menial work, but it paid the bills. He had to boil pasta and had to stand in front of a hot oven for eight hours, so I can imagine it must have taken quite a toll on him. When he set foot in this foreign country to study, he did not imagine doing physical labour. I remember how he would return from work with sweat-drenched hair and lie on his grandmother's lap reading a book in Korean, and I felt some sympathy for him.

Once I started working, it relieved me that I could finally help alleviate his financial burdens. Even though I was new to Canada and had limited English, I encouraged myself with positive affirmations like, *'If I learn and train diligently, I can do well,'* and felt eager to do my job effectively. My role was to make salad, but I had never tasted salad before coming to Canada. I had never seen celery or radish in Korea, and ingredients like cottage cheese seemed unique to me. Eating lettuce or cucumbers in salad dressings made of different ingredients instead of gochujang[7] or doenjang[8] was a fun and new experience for me. Since I enjoyed my job and always worked hard, I often finished my work earlier than others and had some time to relax.

---

[7]   A red chili paste

[8]   A soybean paste

One day, I finished all my tasks early and started helping another employee whose job was to wash dishes. After washing and stacking the dishes, we moved the plates, and I made the mistake of breaking some of them. I was apologetic and flustered, not knowing what to do.

The manager walked up to me and said, "You go home. I'll call you back."

My English still was not adequate, but I understood what those words meant. I went home to tell my husband, and he said that I got "fired." I was confused why he would say I was fired when fire means a burning flame. When I first heard about hot dogs, I thought, confused, '*I heard Canadians don't eat dogs, but do they eat grilled dog meat?*' I would often misunderstand English idioms since they were unfamiliar to me. After hearing that being fired meant being terminated from a job, I replied, "No, he only told me to go home and said they would contact me," and did not believe my husband.

He told me that if I finished my job early and had time left on my shift, I should pretend to be busy. "You only need to do your job," he said. He scolded me for being nosy and trying to help others. For me, it was a given that we should all help one another when we finish our individual tasks, so I could not understand this practice, but I tried to accept that this is the way in Canada.

The next day, I returned to work, and my manager said, "No more work!"

I finally understood that I had lost my job. I was so alien to Canadian culture that I barely understood his words in my broken English. I realized my husband was right and I had been fired.

Tears and sobs came out as soon as I came back home, and I wept. I could not believe that I was told not to come back again. I had never experienced being terminated because I was always competent at any job I performed back home. I was surprised at myself that I got let go for doing such simple labour. My pride was hurt. I could do even more complex tasks in Korea and was consistently recognized for my capabilities. I was in disbelief that

I could not complete such a simple task and had to stop working. It was a hard pill to swallow, and I could not believe it and did not want to believe it. I was bewildered, upset, and thought myself so pathetic and embarrassed that I could not stop crying.

How many immigrants have had their pride wounded in a similar way? I was one of many immigrants living in a country where I did not speak the language but was still trying to prove my worth in a foreign land. I realized then that all these people strived to become successful members of society and we were all competing to be recognized by the general populace as worthy members of the community. This struggle brought me a lot of desolation which I could not share with others unless they experienced it themselves. As an immigrant, I had to start from scratch. Who I was before and how great or terrible I was did not matter anymore; we were reborn in this new land. There was no one to pat my shoulders, give me words of encouragement and pick me up but myself.

This sudden awareness made me want to learn and experience as much as possible. I did not take anything lightly and I tried to absorb everything around me. I became a sponge, and I soaked up all the information that I could. After realizing what I needed to do, my mind slowly silenced into tranquility. In Korea, I achieved all I had through hard work; I always learned passionately and acted wholeheartedly, and I was unafraid of trying new things. This place should be no different, I thought. I must have forgotten how I lived all my life after being coerced into a submissive lifestyle. It was as if I was sleepwalking all this time, but I was finally waking up and coming out of my slumber.

Since I could not expect any support from my husband and had already let go of him emotionally, I thought that I must also let go of my old self. "Even if you give up on him, you must not give up on yourself," I told myself.

Pat, Pat, I consoled my hurt feelings. "This is not the end. I can do better," I whispered to myself. Those words of encouragement healed my soul. "My wings may be folded now, but one day, they will spread wide, and I can soar high in the sky."

Those meaningful phrases gave me strength and the passion to move forward and seek new heights.

The Strength to End Things ...

Once I started believing in myself and that I was the same confident and intelligent person no matter what I was going through, the hard times became more bearable. I recollected my thoughts after concluding that time being sad is time wasted, and I began to adjust to my life in Windsor. No sooner than I started to feel comfortable with my surroundings in Windsor, we got word that we would have to move to another province.

After a year, we moved to Saskatoon for his doctorate. My husband was researching topology then and a well-known professor in that field taught at Saskatoon University. He received a very good scholarship so that we could change provinces quickly. Being uprooted again after such a short while was difficult, but we had to do what was required of us.

Saskatoon is a city located in central Canada on an endless flat field of green; its summers were short, and winters were long and cold. Saskatoon came from a Cree word, Misaskwatomina, which is a sweet purple berry that was abundant in the area. With no mountains in sight, all you could see was miles and miles of flat land. To enjoy leisurely activities in the winter, they would build man-made hills to ski down. In the winter, you could not stand outside for more than five minutes because temperatures would drop to -40 degrees Celsius. Locals would wear thick parkas that covered everything except for their eyes. Because of the cold, buses would arrive every five minutes to transfer people to the

DANDELION OF THAT WINTER

big mall. From there, people boarded the city bus that would take them to their desired destinations.

The snow would fall endlessly in the winter, so residents would shovel a tiny, narrow pathway for a single person to walk through. Starting in August, snow would start to fall and pile up, and by April, there would be snowbanks taller than an average person's height. In May, the weather finally warmed up and all the snow melted simultaneously, often flooding many basements around the city. It was hard to believe that the city would experience flood issues not because of rain but because of snow melting. Since Canada is such a vast country, the environment and lifestyle changed considerably from one end to the other. Saskatoon was very different from Windsor, but familiar fellow students and scholars still surrounded us, so the atmosphere in the world of academia was not much different.

We lived in a student apartment on the university grounds of where he was enrolled in the doctorate program to research and teach. Saskatoon had seven Korean families, and most of them were students. There were no Korean food markets in sight, so we had to rely on a small Chinese grocery store to satisfy our cravings. Meanwhile, we still needed to use cabbage to make kimchi and had to make tofu from scratch. Since there were so few Koreans in town, out-of-city Koreans would flip through the phone book to look for a Korean last name when they visited. This custom must have seemed strange to an outsider, but it was a habit Koreans could not break. We longed for a connection to our past in our new land.

Once, a Korean minister from a missionary church, K, visited us to attend a short-term Christian program. Minister K could not endure his craving for kimchi and contacted us after looking through the phone book to find a person with a Korean last name. We could not imagine how much he must have missed Korean food for him to contact a stranger, so we invited him over for tofu stew and kimchi made of cabbage. Since we did not have Korean cabbage, it was very different from what he had been accustomed to. Still, Minister K gluttonously ate an enormous amount of kimchi, and we worried about his digestion. When it was time for him to leave the city, we gave him a farewell gift. It was a bag made of cowhide. When we reconnected several years later, he welcomed us with open arms and let us know that he still carried around that bag he received from us back then. In those days, there were not many Koreans in Canada, so we helped each other even if we did not know each other very well. We offered assistance, acknowledged each other's needs, and accepted the help we got. It was something we did because we all understood the hardships each of us were facing in a country that was unfamiliar to us in so many ways.

Not long after settling in Saskatoon, an unexpected opportunity found my way. Thanks to an introduction from a Korean staff member working in the biology department, I was able to work as a Teaching Assistant (TA) for first-year biology students and help with their experiments. Finally, I could do something I was experienced in and excelled at. My heart was pounding from the excitement. There were experimental tools that I had never seen before in Korea, so I was as excited as the students. Learning new equipment and procedures that were more advanced than in Korea was not easy, but I enjoyed all the hardships this new challenge had to offer. Microscopes were especially advanced and detailed compared to the ones in Korea, so I often got headaches and tired eyes from looking at them for a short while. Because of the nature of microscopic work, one needed to experiment in a closed-off space, so headaches were an everyday ailment. Nevertheless, these circumstances and language barriers were no longer an obstacle. The expertise I had developed in Korea became the stepping stone for me to improve my skills and prove my worth in Canada.

The head of the biology department observed my efforts and improvements over time and strongly encouraged me to pursue a master's degree. He offered to support my studies as my mentor. He knew that I was hesitant because of my living circumstances

DANDELION OF THAT WINTER

but did not give up on me and instead encouraged me, saying that I could finish the master's degree while continuing my work as a teaching assistant by completing one course per term. It was a fantastic opportunity for me, but I could not forget that I still needed to balance the finances, complete the daily house chores, and continue to be the primary caregiver to my daughter. At the end of each class, the professor would leave a summary of the lesson on the board so I could follow the lecture despite my slow progress in English.

My heart leaped for joy after being recognized for my skills and hard work at long last. From the beginning, I wished to come to Canada to study and return home with successful accomplishments that I could boast about. Along with my husband's doctorate, this seemed to be within arm's reach. My personal philosophy that if I do not give up and work hard, then I will succeed, seemed to be proving itself. My outlook changed for the better and I felt like the whole world seemed to shine so brightly.

If one could fly, perhaps this is how it felt. When I returned home, I announced this great news to my husband. Unsurprisingly, it was met with his cold expressions and a colder silence. I froze up. Unsure of what exactly I did wrong, I glanced at him timidly. I did not know what upset him and felt anxious about giving up this dream. He looked over with a cold glance and said to me,

"Why did you come here? Did you come to help me or to study?" The unexpected interrogation made me forget my words. "Sure. If that is the case, you can study. I will do the housework." His tone was sarcastic enough to make me wince.

'He is unhappy. No, he is angry,' I thought. My heart, that had been blossoming like spring flowers, withered away in an instant. His frigid personality could bring down a mountain never mind my blossoming heart.

I forced myself to remember that his success was my success, and his dreams were essentially my dreams. Every time he was recognized in his field and had the opportunity to grow, I was truly happy and looked out for him to see what he needed. My duty as a wife was to follow and help him achieve his desires which I could do because of fidelity between one human and another. I realized then that my growth and dreams were hindrances to him. For him, it was expected of me to sacrifice myself and support him to achieve his success, yet I could not expect the same in return. My dreams and desires were a burden for him. They would only get in the way of his success and that kind of obstacle was unwelcome.

I put my heart, my soul and my identity aside and just accepted everything as it was. I was there to help him, and my wishes would have to come last if at all. I also thought to myself that he came first in my life, my daughter was second and my needs had to be sacrificed for now. I naively thought, *'If I do not give up, an opportunity will one day come again so let's look after him first.'* So, I made up my mind. I would do what was expected of me and play the part of the dutiful wife. In retrospect, it was the easy way out, but at the time, it seemed like the right thing to do. I wanted to show honesty, respect and faithfulness to my husband by supporting him to achieve his goals in any way I could.

I suppose if this happened today, the situation would not be much different. I believe that it is extremely difficult to achieve something without the help of your family- especially your partner. But today, perhaps partners take turns sacrificing for one another. That is the difference. Today, partners build an environment of trust in their relationship where they both feel confident and secure in each other's commitment to their marriage. Back then, women made all the sacrifices. The notion was that even if a wife was more talented than her husband, she must hide her aptitudes and not show off. Thus, I peacefully accepted another pause in my life once again.

The anxious tension between us seemed to have impacted our daughter's mental health as she found it difficult to stay apart from me. Perhaps she knew from intuition that I, her mother, was her only string so she held on to me as tightly as possible to avoid letting go of that connection she saw as her lifeline. All

DANDELION OF THAT WINTER

she ever felt from her father was coldness and neglect. Her poor little heart must have felt frozen. She must have looked for some form of warmth to melt her heart, making her snuggle deeper in her mother's arms. When I would leave her in the care of the babysitter to head out for work, she would wail and cry with all her might until I returned home. Even when I sent her off with her favourite food, she would only eat if I was within her sight. One morning, as I was busy getting ready, I found her hidden in the corner of my closet. She hugged my clothes tightly and wept. Seeing that sight of her made me feel selfish for following my dreams while my daughter needed me more than ever. The guilt I felt daily, leaving for work, was unexplainable.

Before leaving Korea, my husband suggested that I leave our daughter at our in-laws. His reason was that without the responsibility of a child, both he and I could study more easily and live more comfortably. I could not even think of leaving our child behind. I was even unsure about leaving our child behind in the middle of the countryside with our mother-in-law, where I knew no one could hurt her, but I also thought that it was wrong to abandon my child even if it was for the financial advancement of our family which would one day benefit her as well. But money was not going to make my daughter forgive me for leaving her to be raised by her grandparents.

It seemed that no one wanted me to pursue my dreams and ambitions. I had no choice but to stop working towards my goals because I lacked the support of those nearest and dearest to me. I do not know what is more courageous: conflicting with family members over chasing my dreams or stopping my life's ambitions for others. I am sure some would say that I was too young and inexperienced to realize that opportunity does not come around that often in life. Perhaps they were right in assuming this. One thing was for sure, I did not blame anyone back then, and I calmly and collectedly decided to just relax. That was not an easy decision. To stop, to wait. To level my heart and let go of all my desires. All this required courage and I desperately needed that courage. Bravery was needed to not collapse under despair. And back then, I was brave. Like a warrior.

A Stone Hidden in the Mist ...

It appears that when life is surrounded by fog, you do not know where and when you will trip over a rock. As per my husband's wish and for the sake of our daughter, I declined Dr. B's offer, who was the head of the biology department at that time. I also resigned from working at school. My husband understood my decision, our daughter seemed happier, and everything seemed to go smoothly. Until one day, Dr. B came to our student apartment looking for me. As the chief of the biology department, he did not understand why someone with such great potential would give up such a promising offer and resign from a position where they could succeed and continuously learn. There was no way of contacting me once I resigned so he approached my husband at the school office to find our address and came to speak with me at our student apartment.

I felt sorry for disappointing him when he entrusted me with such incredible opportunities. I was too embarrassed to admit my husband would not allow me to study, so I made up a lame excuse about why I had to resign. Dr. B's intention was to convince me otherwise. He was not going to accept my resignation without some discussion. Without inviting him inside, I exchanged words over the intercom. I knew well what it felt like to lose a student with great potential, and I understood his disappointment, however, my husband and my daughter were more important to me, so I turned him away.

The aftermath of Dr. B's visit was far too great. My husband would use ridiculous reasons to interrogate me. He asked what relationship I had with Dr. B and even suspected I had slept with him.

"Did you sleep with that punk? If you didn't sleep with him then why would a Canadian man come and look for a married Asian woman whom he has not known for too long? There is no way. You better tell me the truth." He yelled.

He used primitive language and denounced me; it was humiliating. I could not believe he would even think of suspecting me of such things. I no longer wanted to live while being accused of being that kind of woman. Just how low could he get and how much longer could I endure these unjustified outbreaks and accusations? Everything was terrible and insufferable. His verbal attacks showered on me while I sat there like a wood block. I tried hard not to fall as this fog storm passed through my life, so I just stood there like a tree, like a rock, unmoving as if I were dead. I stopped thinking. I laid still as if I was dead, just to survive.

My daughter stuck close to me with anxious eyes and pressed her head in my lap. We hugged each other tightly as if to not lose each other while walking through a thick blanket of fog with no visibility. We did not know how many stones were hidden to trip me in this mist and I could not estimate how many falls I could endure. Up until that moment, my life was full of hope and brilliance, and suddenly I was walking through an inescapable fog. My happiness and sadness depended on my husband's feelings and actions as he made all the important decisions in my life.

The faint ray of sunshine shining through the cracks of clouds went away just like that. That is how quickly hope disappeared. On a cold winter's day close to Christmas, we found out in the hospital that I was pregnant. It was as if the second child in my womb felt that I was about to give up and needed to let their presence be known so that I could hang on for them. It was not like the pure happiness that I had felt when my daughter came to me, but this child's emergence gave me the support that I needed.

DANDELION OF THAT WINTER

News of our second child was the only sweet present during Christmas when I felt nothing but bitterness.

My husband intended to complete his doctorate studies in Saskatoon but had to halt his studies unexpectedly. His supervisor went on a sabbatical to an American university and was on leave for two years, so my husband decided to find a temporary job and travelled to Toronto alone. He ended up in Ottawa and found a job with his professor's recommendation.

I gave birth to a beautiful boy in Saskatoon on my own. Perhaps because my son wanted to meet his mother or was curious about the world, the labour lasted only an hour after I arrived at the hospital. My body was too weak at this point, and I needed to be hospitalized for a week. Since my husband was in Ottawa, Dr. Shin's family took care of our daughter. We were in a difficult situation, so we asked for help which we seldom did. Despite knowing it would be difficult, they happily accepted and looked after our daughter. They had children as well and often gave us clean, looked-after, hand-me-down clothes, but I never got to thank them properly. It remains in my heart as a regret that I could never really express my gratitude for all their support at the time that I needed it most.

It was only the end of August, but winter had begun already. Snow laid across the endless prairie like white satin and took away all my warmth while I hugged my son in my arms. It was a cold winter. My husband arrived in Ottawa with more than enough qualifications and found a job without any problem. That overqualification made it difficult for him to get along with other employees. He had a strenuous time because he could not get along with people at work because of his challenging and problematic personality. He could not accept that he had to work under a younger person with less education and stubbornly rejected the government job.

It would not have been difficult to find a job in Korea back then with his academic background. At that point, some universities back home had already offered him a job in a teaching position.

However, he did not wish to return to Korea. Although our life may have been a poor and arduous one, but compared to Korea, Canada was overall more sophisticated in social settings and had elevated living standards. It was not too difficult to understand why he did not wish to return home.

Post-war Korea went through a turbulence of political differences and conflicts, and he lost his father as a child in the middle of all that. His father was a police officer. And in the middle of the chaos when everyone was pointing their guns at each other, he lost his father and experienced abject poverty. So perhaps it was never his intention to abandon the opportunities laid before him and return to a wounded Korea in the first place.

Ottawa is the capital city of Canada and is known for being clean and peaceful. Most of the city's residents work in public institutions, as middle-tier officials, or as accountants and lawyers for those individuals. Due to its demographics, the city has a calm, stable, and relaxed atmosphere. Across the river is Quebec, a predominantly French-speaking region, where the city is adorned with trees along the river. In the winter, the river freezes, and it is enjoyable to watch people skating across it.

After quitting his job, my husband did not have much money saved so he accepted a position as a translator at a newspaper company. From there, he started working as a gas station manager which was a gateway to working in an entirely new field unrelated to academics or education. Working at a small gas station in Ottawa was a brand-new challenge for us and it brought significant changes to our lives. We had never imagined working anywhere other than a school or educational institution, so it was a new experience for us. Compared to relying on scholarships to maintain our living, he felt joy from working in a greasy work suit and earning a wage based on his hard manual work.

Not long after moving to Ottawa, I became pregnant again. Sadly, I could not be happy about expecting this child. I was scared that the child might feel my hesitancy. I did not want them to feel unwanted but if I was going to be honest with myself, I truly was depressed that I was with child once more. My husband was impartial to the news. I knew he was conservative about showing affection or responsibility towards his children as a father, but his impartialness disappointed me a lot. Had he shown excitement, perhaps I would have not been so depressed about expecting another child. I felt as if it was my fault that our children would grow up without experiencing fatherly love. I could not feel entirely happy about bringing this child into the world when I knew of these obstacles in our marriage.

My body was already weak and frail by the time I birthed our third child. There was severe edema below my knees, and Dr. Grant, who was looking after my health, suggested that I be admitted to the hospital. It was not an easy decision for me as I needed to look after our children and oversee the housework. Dr. Grant graciously offered to visit our home once a week to examine me after hearing about my circumstances. He did not mind coming to a messy and rundown home and always treated me with compassion and kindness. I am thankful for him to this day. Perhaps exactly because of these compassionate human beings in various parts of my life that I was able to persevere through the hard times no matter how hard it got.

During my third trimester, an acquaintance of mine invited me over to her place after work for some aged kimchi since she knew I was closer to the due date and saw how exhausted I was from work. The words 'aged kimchi' was more than enough for me to stop what I was doing and go to their place to have a meal. I had lost my appetite from morning sickness at this point and could not eat much food throughout the day. Despite the sickness, the kimchi was so delicious and reminded me so much of home that I could not swallow while trying to hold back the tears. It was heavenly bliss. The consequence of eating aged kimchi and a meal was more brutal than I had expected. I got home much later than usual, and my husband refused to open the doors for me out of anger. I had to wait outside in the cold Canadian winter until he calmed down. There was nothing I could do other than hold on to my big stomach tightly to keep warm. He never opened the door. It was the children who opened the door for me after some time.

My hands and feet were frozen, and he lashed out at me with another tantrum, but I was able to endure it when I remembered the taste of home. That meal was like a helping hand that appeared just when I tripped over a rock and could not get back up.

We soon found stability from running the gas station. Like other immigrant families, we worked hard each day with our daughter and two sons born thereafter. After work, my husband usually hung out with his friends or visited his seniors from Korea on the weekends. That is when he also began to see other women. It did not bother me in the slightest. In fact, instead of being upset that he was having an affair, I would buy him expensive suits from Burberry and other fine places to encourage him to go out more often. If he came home late, our children and I were free from verbal and physical abuse for a longer time. It was like I was buying some temporary freedom.

One afternoon, a Canadian couple walked up to us and asked if we were Koreans. Their children were adopted from Korea and wanted to eat something specific, but they did not know what it was called and asked for our help. We agreed to help and the next day they showed up with two little girls who looked to be around the age of seven. The girls wanted persimmon. Right away I told their Canadian mother that the girls wanted to eat persimmon. They responded with a bright smile, thanked me, and headed off to buy persimmon. The family looked so warm and happy. My heart ached, thinking they must have missed the taste of home even at a young age. I was not too different from those little girls as I also experienced homesickness and missed the taste of home. Those two girls should be about sixty by now. I wonder where they are and how they are doing, and if they still crave persimmon around the fall.

During another evening, an unfamiliar Canadian couple visited the gas station while we were closing and asked us which country we were from. I looked confused as I did not know why they were asking, and they explained that they had a $10 dollar bet on our ethnicity. My husband regularly wore his greasy work suit, and compared to him, I always worked in clean clothes. The husband of the Canadian couple bet that I was Japanese while the wife bet my husband was indigenous. I told them that they both lost the bet since we are Koreans, and they both let out a cheerful laugh. I often think about how rare encounters with immigrants were back then and now are very commonplace.

Ordinary days went by when our fourth child came to us. My husband was enraged at the news. He stated very clearly how much he did not want the child. I was also mentally divorced from him at that point and could not welcome the child wholeheartedly. I was unsure whether I could give this child the love they deserved, especially when I remembered how difficult and stressful the process of carrying our third child was.

He berated me thinking that I tried to use pregnancy as an excuse to not work. I never stopped working, even throughout carrying our third child- before labour and after giving birth. He continued complaining about how unfair it was for him to be the sole financial supporter, and that I must work right up to my due date, he insisted. I was exhausted both physically and mentally. I already had three children to protect and raise, so I was barely hanging on. I did not have the heart to bring another soul to live through this cruel and insufferable life with my husband. I also was not confident that I could survive this fourth labour. The guilt of letting go of this life would haunt me for the rest of my life but I just could not do it. And my husband's cold stare made me realize that this sin was meant to be carried solely by me.

The hospitals in Ottawa refused to perform an abortion surgery because I was already four months pregnant, so I asked around for a hospital in Toronto and went by myself. My husband did not have any concerns for me and this poor condemned soul. He absolved himself from any responsibility regarding this case and left me alone with the burden of going to Toronto and undergoing the heart-wrenching abortion process all by myself.

When I needed a guardian at the hospital to accompany me after the surgery, I had to ask my acquaintance to be there for me. The doctors informed me that once I have this abortion, I must also have a contraceptive surgery, so I had to have a laparotomy and tubal ligation to tie up my fallopian tubes. I went through two harrowing and gut-wrenching surgeries on my own. It was a lonely and regretful time for me.

I had to let go of this unborn life alone, without my husband. Instead of returning home with a newborn baby, I returned with an everlasting lump that would remind me of the serious and tragic decision I made. My soul felt so empty and broken, and tears were flooding my face. All my senses slowly died away after that. A woman without any facial expressions- that is who I was. I could not feel anything and therefore could not express anything. I was stuck in a void with no senses present. After a while, whenever I saw a pregnant woman or a baby, I felt immense pain as if my heart was ripping apart. Even now I have moments where the sudden gush of guilt overwhelms my heart and body, causing me to break down. Going through an abortion is not easy. It has life altering consequences but at the time, I could not bring another life into our broken and unstable home.

Despite all this, I returned to my normal routine. My husband looked at me as if nothing happened in the first place, I passed him without feeling and continued to do my part around the house. I continued to live walking down a pathless road. Once you live through it all, there should be an end in sight, but for me, my hardship seemed endless. I still had three children I needed to bring up and they continued to smile at me, giving me a reason to live on.

My children's little hands were the ones helping me up when I would fall from walking through the thick fog with no clear path and tripping over stones. Those six shiny eyes were the lights leading me in the pitch-black darkness and allowing me to step forward over obstacles. They were a source of strength that helped me get back up whenever I was down. They were the steps walking beside me cheering me on. Because of them, I could walk through the fog and continue walking even after falling several times. No matter how thick the mist might be, it would lift once the sun rose, so I needed to continue walking straight towards the rising sun. I needed to walk on no matter how long it would take.

Looking up at the Sky in the Fog...

After garnering some investment money from the gas station business, he purchased an old house to renovate with his friends which he resold. This profitable investment allowed him to save enough money to buy a convenience store on the outskirts of Toronto. The convenience store came with a second-floor apartment that was big enough for our family. I could work while watching over our children on the second floor and this way of life helped me feel a little less stressed and more at ease. He also felt financially stable enough to purchase a golf membership with his friends and began to spend more time outside of our domicile.

He would do nothing but complain whenever he returned to our residence. The mood in our home would often turn sour because of him so I would encourage him to go out to avoid arguing with him. Since he was not around to demand homecooked meals, the children and I would eat instant food like burgers for dinner on days he would come home late. I could not leave the store to cook dinner for the children, but for them eating instant food occasionally was quite a joy compared to eating our traditional meals.

Although it was not spoken about openly, I think my husband noticed that the silence and distance settling in between he and I was a form of criticism toward him. I was expressing how I felt without uttering a word. He could not have been aloof to the fact that I felt more comfortable without him around. Perhaps that was why he would make snarky comments about the food I made or mess it up by adding water or random sauces here and there. He would throw trash randomly around the house as he walked around or cut the carpet with scissors to show his disdain in a sinister way. Sometimes he would take out the lamp plugs around the house because he detested seeing me read a book or write after closing the store. Once, he even unplugged the fridge and we had a small flood in our home the next day. He would pull these stunts as if he was a little boy throwing a tantrum. I refrained from showing any reaction as a way of condemning him. If he wanted to act like a toddler, I would treat him as one, I thought and so I did.

No matter what he did or what names he called me, I responded with silence, ignoring his call for attention. Slowly, I became used to his ongoing mental and physical abuses. It hurt my pride to argue with him and fight back so I chose not to respond to his provocations. There was no point in engaging in a no-win scenario. It did not matter how irrational or how violent his tantrums became; I did not give him a single bit of recognition. It was liberating! Looking back, I chose to avoid having big arguments with him perhaps to drive him to a lonelier place and elicit more outrageous behaviour from him. Whenever I faced him with silence, he would yell at me with a face turned red with rage.

"You are thinking about how terrible I am, aren't you? It's written all over your face!" he would say.

Thinking back on it now, I wonder if his intention behind his attention-seeking actions was for me to notice him. I once read that little children throw tantrums to draw their parents' attention upon themselves when they feel deprived of love and neglected. It is a phenomenon commonly found among children who do not know how to communicate their needs for attention and love in a healthy way. My husband and I were brought up in a generation where we believed that love would eventually develop and grow after we got married so we did not feel the need to express our love for one another. It was given that parents would love their children, so it was considered normal not to convey it verbally to them. We lived through a time when people were not very vocal about expressing their love for their partner or siblings. "Do we necessarily need to say it out loud? We all know we love each other even without saying it." That's what we would say, but truthfully, we were a generation that did not know how to show affection to each other using language.

My husband must have also experienced hardships and loneliness during our marriage. He needed comfort as well while he worked through these uncomfortable feelings. A feeling of emptiness visited him one day when he was busy working. He must have missed the unconditional love his parents gave him when he was a child. Unfortunately, he did not know the mature way to vocalize and process those feelings. No one taught him how and he did not want to learn. I also did not try to overcome our issues and try to be the problem solver. Instead, I did not fight back fiercely, and by not standing up to him, I may have caused him to feel neglected. We were none the wiser as we lacked the understanding of what it was like to live as a married couple, and we did not know how to resolve common disagreements among ourselves. We were fools who did not know how to fix our own marital problems.

In our generation, when we would come across complications, we would just endure them until the problem resolved itself naturally. Divorce was not an option just because a married couple was going through some turmoil. Couples therapy or marital counselling was not widely available or affordable back then. We could not think of any other option to help resolve our problems. Looking back on it, I feel sorry for our generation. My husband and I both believed that one day things would change, and we just waited as all the storms passed us by. I thought that if I dug my heel deep into the ground and endured everything, all would eventually be resolved. I believed that my husband would one day recognize my patience and change his ways, so I endured and suffered.

DANDELION OF THAT WINTER

One day, my daughter commented about this foolish endurance I maintained for many years,

"Mom, it's difficult for a person to change after age forty. It is not that they don't want to change, but they lack the internal strength to change themselves by that age."

I thought she might have been right. After waiting for my husband to change for many years with no noticeable difference, I sometimes wondered if he knew at all how to change.

At the time when our marriage was situated at the centre of a storm where calm prevailed temporarily, my husband's younger brother and his wife who lived nearby, were also experiencing problems of their own. My brother-in-law was married to one of my previous students from Korea. I last saw her when she graduated but we still exchanged letters for some time afterwards. My brother-in-law looked through my letters and found a picture of her, and without letting me know he must have started writing to her. Neither me nor my husband knew that the two had begun their relationship through their exchange of letters and pictures.

It sounds like a tale from the olden days, but parcel marriages were still quite common back then. Koreans living in Canada, no matter their gender, quite often wanted to marry other Koreans because they spoke the same language and shared the same culture. Being introduced to other Koreans overseas through acquaintances was not uncommon, and since it was not cheap to fly overseas back then, people would be set up through pictures. Many Koreans opted for this type of marriage because they could have a partnership with someone to which they could easily relate. The wish to marry someone from home was quite a normal and popular wish.

People's intentions and purpose is sometimes tough to figure out, even after living with someone every day. My husband objected sternly when his brother announced his marriage. He did not understand how one could know someone well enough to marry without meeting them in person or exchanging words and disapproved of their marriage. He worried that his future sister-in-law had a history of tuberculosis in the family and objected because she did not seem to have an easygoing personality based on the angle of her eyes in the picture. The idiom, *do not judge a book by its cover*, did not exist in my husband's vernacular.

I also advised his brother to think about this proposed union because I wanted to present myself and my husband as a united front, but we could not stop two adults who had already made their decision. My husband and I knew how important it was to know one another and be committed to the marriage through our own experience, so we could not help but worry at the news of their marriage. I was unsure how much they had expressed and honestly shared about themselves in their letters without ever meeting in person.

My brother-in-law was a sincere and hard-working young man. In my memory, my pupil also had great grades in school and was well known for being a great singer. I knew how two seemingly easy-going, yet different people can change when they meet one another, and could not help but feel uneasy. I just prayed that everything would go well for them.

My pupil arrived in Canada and seemed as if she was expecting a life right out of the movies. Her suitcase was packed with fine clothes suited for parties. She soon realized that these clothes were not practical for her life in Canada, and she began to feel fed up living with a husband who worked in greasy overalls all day. She was a nurse back in Korea, so she often thought about her life among doctors working in clean hospital gowns. She could not get used to the sight of her own husband working at a gas station in a grimy jumpsuit.

They had two children together and this added to their differences instead of unifying them. My brother-in-law would often be too busy with work but on the other hand his wife enjoyed attending church gatherings and going out more often. My sister-in-law was a great singer who entered the Toronto Korean choir and began leaving home more frequently with different schedules filling up her weekly calendar. Rumours began to circle around about my sister-in-law. Whenever the rumours would surface that his wife was seeing other men, he suffered greatly but did not do anything about it. Although they were our family, we could not interfere with their problems without them asking for our help first. We could not monitor and scold them as they were also adults, so we often observed them with worry and sadness. We could not do much. My husband helped his brother in different ways to stabilize their financial livelihoods. I looked after our nephews and nieces to support my sister-in-law in her endeavours as she wished they could build a stable family home as soon as possible.

The couples of our generation believed that whatever happens in a marriage is their own problem. They did not think to talk about their difficult situation with outsiders or see a specialist to get help. Most people would just tolerate their complications and hope they would pass with time. I also did not talk about my turmoil to my family members to get assistance. Those who did not know what was happening in our marriage often told me I was lucky to have such a fantastic husband. Although he never hugged his own children, he was kind and gentle to other children, so it made sense for people to think accordingly.

I would stifle a cry inside and smile on the outside when I heard such compliments about my husband. I did not want other people to know how I was treated at home, and I did not want them to know his true self. My pride did not allow for the father of my children to be the topic of local gossip, and I did not want our children to be hurt by meaningless chatter. At those who were telling me how happy I seemed to be or how fortunate I was, I just smiled. Even if I was crying tears of blood on the inside, I smiled silently on the outside.

For all I know, many couples live lives in contrast to what the outside world sees. There may be a lot of other couples out there who have unresolved problems festering in their lives but have never uttered a cry for help from outsiders. They could also be too embarrassed to show their imperfect life to others, so they suffer by themselves. My brother-in-law's family may have had problems of their own that others could not even predict. Perhaps they were also walking through a foggy road, trying to battle a messy drawback without being able to ask for help.

It was a life where one would fall repeatedly in a single day and continue to move on. I innocently lived on thinking that watching my children eat was the meaning of my life. This thought was truly sincere as I thought if my children are healthy at least, then my job as a mother is complete. I was sure there were other people out there just like me who continued to live without looking at how festering their wounds had become and sacrificed their lives for their children.

We had to deal with our own pain alone, so understanding the pains of others was too cumbersome. Everyone was standing in a cloud of mist, unable to see one another as we looked around. Since we could not see in front of ourselves, we could not see the obstacles others faced so we just waited for a ray of light to come out of the sky to help us find the way. We could feel our proximity to each other but without a loud cry of, "I am here, help me," no one knew where you could be found and that was the fog we were stuck in. And just like that, tragedy crept up on us without a sound.

Shattered...

It was a busy morning like any other day. I prepared our children for school and my husband went for a round of golf with his friends early in the morning. I restocked our shelves alone and got ready to open the store. Through the murky window, I felt the May sunshine upon me and hurried to be ready for our opening time as my nephews ran in looking for water. I grabbed a drink for them while wondering why they had run since we were quite far away from each other's houses. That is when I heard something unbelievable coming from my nephew's mouth.

"Mom and Dad are dead. There's a lot of blood. We were too scared and ran away!"

"You brats shouldn't say stuff like that. You should not say that your parents are dead, even as a joke." I said in a huff, upset that they would joke about their parents in that way.

I scolded the children for saying such menacing words without ever imagining that their words may be true.

"No, Auntie, it's real! Mom and Dad are dead. And there's a lot of blood."

That's when I realized something terrible happened.

"Really? There's really blood? Are they really dead?" I asked the questions I did not wish to hear the answers to. I felt the blood leave my body, and all my hair stand on end. I have never been that scared in my life- It was frightening. The children repeated the word "dead" with pale faces, but I muttered to myself, "No, it cannot be... The children must have seen something they misinterpreted like in a nightmare."

I forgot how I called the police and what I said to them, but I could only hug my two nephews to stop myself from shaking and hope the children were mistaken.

The police arrived. We got into the police car and drove to our brother-in-law's house and saw other policemen were already there with yellow police lines placed around the building to prevent others from entering. I did not know what to think, I was numb. Words were unable to come out of my mouth. All I could say was, "Are they alive or dead?" whenever I came across people who looked like police.

Police responded with uncertainty, so I held on to that ray of hope and went to the police station with the children. I do not know how I managed to sit there and wait through the entire police investigation. I remember some people in the office would bring food for their children in case they were hungry and suggested some food or drink for me, but I could barely manage to drink water. I just sat still without even swallowing. I answered the police officers' questions as if I were a robot, and the question, "What happened?" continued to ring loud in my head.

I was unaware of how much time had passed. An officer walked through the door, and I looked up at him, waiting for an answer and holding onto another strand of hope.

"Are they alive or dead?" I repeated for the umpteenth time.

"I am sorry, they're gone."

Something white and foggy filled my head and covered my eyes. My body began to sink to the ground against my will. I was unsure who helped me up or if I even received any help as I continued to sit on the chair. My heart ripped to a thousand pieces as unfathomable grief overcame me and a well of tears were running down my face. It was so heartbreaking that they would leave just like that, and I felt utterly sorry. I did not know how to express this sorrow; I could only beat my body until it bruised to relieve my agony. I had to experience this moment alone since I did not know which golf course my husband went to and could not contact him.

The police sent our nephews to a temporary shelter, and I returned home in a police car. My children returned home from school, and it was unclear how that afternoon passed. Every moment was blurred into one another. The extreme shock and sorrow burdened me greatly and it was difficult for me to keep my thoughts straight.

My husband returned home late at night from the golf course. After hearing this rupturing news, he just remained silent. He did not move an inch even after hearing that his beloved brother ended his wife's life and eventually took his own. He was unsure if he should believe the story or it was not to be believed, but he did not move. I could only imagine how he must have felt based on how I was feeling. He lost his dear brother. I spent the night in a daze, unsure of what was happening, and hugged my children for comfort. That is when he walked up to me. He did not usually drink but I could smell the alcohol on his breath.

"You killed my brother. You are just a stranger to me since we don't live with each other as man and wife, and my brother is my family that has the same blood as me, but you killed him. He wouldn't have died if you had not introduced that woman to him. Because of you, my brother is dead."

He began to scream like a maniac, and I could not do anything to stand up against his rage, all I could do was cry. His words brought guilt to me. What if they really did die because of me? The guilt began to tear my heart into smithereens. If It was not for me, they would have never had the chance to meet and they would not be dead. These vain regrets ripped my heart apart.

He poured his sorrows and pain upon me with toxic words and verbal abuse while hammering a nail into my heart. It was a long night. I thought the morning would never come. This was what hell felt like, I surmised. In a room filled with darkness, I needed to endure every recollection of the day's events again and again by myself. I wanted to end my life. I could not live through the torment one more minute. There were a lot of mixed feelings flooding in. I pitied the dead, missed them, and felt guilty, and countless other feelings that made me feel as though I was drowning. The emotions swarmed me and took over my body and brain. I did not wish to live anymore that day. As harsh as his baseless criticism and blame landed upon me and as much as his rage and misery lashed out at me, sadness took a big and heavy chunk of my heart. I slowly withered away that night, unable to support the weight of the sorrow. It was a time filled with silent cries and despair.

My sister-in-law's last words were stuck in my head. She called a bit after midnight the night before. She apologized for missing my daughter's birthday party, but I told her not to fret about it and I also conveyed to her that I was worried about her and advised her to go home immediately for the sake of her family.

"I'm sorry, Jeong Ae," she responded.

That night, I also received a frantic call from my brother-in-law worried about his wife's whereabouts. I told him not to be alarmed and to call me once his wife got home no matter how late it was.

Eventually, I found out my brother-in-law was waiting on their fourteenth-floor balcony and saw his wife get out of another man's car and assumed she was with him all night. We already knew that she was seeing another man. We tried to stop her from continuing the affair by suggesting they bring our mother-in-law to Canada and live with her.

One day, my brother-in-law saw a stranger sitting on his sofa when he returned home late around 11 p.m. He asked the stranger who he was and why he was in his house at such a late hour. He responded, "You can say those words now, but you won't be able to once you are separated." My husband and I decided that we needed to put an end to this relationship after hearing about this encounter from my brother-in-law. We began talking to my sister-in-law about putting an end to her extramarital relationship. But our attempts were futile.

DANDELION OF THAT WINTER

It seemed that seeing his wife get out of another man's car must have triggered his anger. Mulling this over and over in his head drove him insane even after ending the call with me late at night. Many questions puzzled me, and I could not breathe from pitying their lives and worrying about the children left behind. My brother-in-law's desperate voice while searching for his wife that night clouded my mind. The voice of my sister-in-law saying, "I'm sorry, Jeong Ae," lingered in my ear.

The next day, our family was sitting in the eye of a big powerful storm. The winds of gossip pushed us around and waves of harsh and cruel words from others left us confused. It was as if we were standing in the eye of a hurricane, its reach was vast, covering the entire world in dust. I was stuck in the whirlwind, swept up in the twirling tornado, spinning and spinning without an end in sight. At times I thought the storm was subsiding a bit, only for it to pick up speed again and again. You would not know how jarring and tyrannical those days were unless you experienced it yourself. There are no words to explain the judgement and accusations I came up against from community members.

The female church members of my sister-in-law's church were particularly harsh with me. I was a columnist at the Joseon Daily and they directed all their blame and allegations towards me. They berated me, saying I caused this misery, for neglecting our in-laws while calling for more compassion in my writing. I heard rumours that they even banded together to look for me and beat me up. I had to experience being labeled as culpable in the death of my sister-in-law by the Korean community, and at home I had to put up with my husband's grief-stricken anger.

My sister-in-law's family back in Korea also sent me angry letters asking how I could introduce a murderer to their daughter and held me responsible for her death. I could not eat or sleep. I began to lose weight drastically and looked like a bag of bones, but it was still too difficult for me to eat or swallow anything. I knew then what it meant when Koreans would say it felt as if you were chewing sand. Several days and weeks went by without eating much and in time my legs began to shake, and I could not walk easily.

He started to drink every day after his brother's death. He never indulged in alcohol before. Every day he used his intoxicated state of mind to make me and our children kneel in front of him while scolding me for allegedly killing his brother. If any of the children dozed off, he threatened to throw pepper water in their eyes and ordered them to kneel correctly. If he was unsatisfied even after that, he would pull out a knife and threaten to kill me. After going through multiple cycles of abuse, he would fall asleep first and that's when we finally found enough calm to nod off.

One day I could not tolerate the endless abuse and finally said to him, "I'll kill myself. I'll go out and kill myself. If you kill me, that is too great of a pain for our children to bear. We can't let our children go through that, especially after your brother killed his wife. If I go out and kill myself then you don't have to spend money hiring the mafia."

I could not bear to kill myself with our children watching and I told him I would go out to die, and he held the knife closer to me. I resigned.

"Let's just die right here. That's what this human really wants." He threatened, holding out a knife.

I laid flat on the kitchen floor and waited for him to kill me quickly. He held the blade high above me and slammed it down. The knife struck the wooden floor next to my head. Finally, the knife fiasco had come to an end. For a long time after that incident, our eldest son began to hide all the knives whenever it was close to my husband's home coming. It was a nightmarish time for us. My husband, me, our children, and our nephews were all hurt, in pain, and suffering. Still there was no consolation anywhere around us.

The people that surrounded us were quick to gossip and blame us instead of offering comfort while our family steeped in sorrow. There was only shallow curiosity and imprudent blame. We were breathing, but it felt as if we were drowning. The Canadian government ordered us to start therapy. This court order was the public officials' way of worrying about and caring for us when we were broken mentally and physically from this tragic incident. After the first therapy session, it was assessed that my husband and nephews would need two years of psychological therapy, unlike me and our three children. He argued that he was not mentally disturbed and refused the government-ordered therapy sessions. There were many calls to convince him to see a therapist thereafter, but he continued to refuse them, and it got to the point where he needed to go to court but nothing was finalized. My husband may have wanted to treat his pain by abusing me instead of going to treatment.

We had to decide where and how our young nephews would live during this time of sorrow and unjust harassment by the people around us. Listening to laws we had never heard about before, he and I realized how unfamiliar this country we have been living in was to us. Yes, we were immigrants and had lived here for quite some time by that point, but we were living an ordinary life and did not know much about civil laws or policies because we never needed to learn about them before. We were always law-abiding citizens that never got mixed up with the police or needed to hire lawyers. We were new to Canadian laws and there was a big gap in our knowledge from not just language barriers and inexperience with local laws but also from cultural differences. We were new to the legal system, and we did not know how to navigate it. We felt defeated.

Of course, we tried to raise our nephews as our own. However, adopting our nephews was not a simple thing of just packing their belongings and bringing them to our place. It was only possible after we were able to prove that we could support these children within the standards set by Canadian law, and they granted us approval. Endless rounds of counseling, interviews, and document evaluations followed.

The laws in this unfamiliar land stated that we did not have the qualifications to raise our nephews in a small two-bedroom apartment above a convenience store. My husband grew weary from fighting against the Canadian government to prove he could bring up his nephews. Without his help, it was impossible for me to stand against legislations and prove that I could support and bring up these children.

My husband had come here to study without any help, and he could not achieve what he aspired to because of financial pressures. He was not too eager to adopt his nephews in this challenging time. Meanwhile, the Canadian government's requirements were too unrealistic for us to achieve as they ordered us to move to a four-bedroom house, and I, a sole caregiver, could not work for more than four hours a day. The clause stating that we needed to fulfill all of this and decide on everything within six months became an irresistible excuse for him. It was a moment when we began to miss the Korean standard of duty and compassion since they would not have compelled us to do much as long as the children had a place to sleep.

Dr. Cho, a provincial minister of the Ontario government, visited us several times offering to take care of our nephews as his own. Many Koreans looked down on me and hated me, but a handful of people like Dr. Cho and his wife, understood the situation we were in and offered help. However, after enduring a lot of gossip in the Korean community, my husband and I did not want to leave the children in a Korean household. In Korean culture, it was common for children to inherit the fault or weakness of their parents, and we wished to protect these children from experiencing that. My husband also said that we cannot give the Korean community more opportunity to tell tales about us since they love to talk about others.

In the end, a Canadian foster parent took our nephews in. Because of this, the Korean community berated me even more fiercely. It did not matter to them what the truth was or what our circumstances were. They were too busy making up different theories to throw more ill feelings and bad wishes at me. I started

DANDELION OF THAT WINTER

to breathe and consume the foul words as if they were water and air.

"How could they call themselves human beings and not take care of those poor children," said one.

"She deserves to die," said another.

"What a wench."

Our community labelled me with primitive and foul words. My husband was too humiliated to reveal that the government would not allow us to bring his nephews home for financial reasons and instead shifted all the blame to me in front of all the Koreans who were waiting for more reasons to condemn me. He could not accept the burden brought forth on our family and said things like, "my wife didn't want to bring in the children because she didn't want to take care of them," to shield himself from any blame. My husband chose to lie and tell a fabricated story because the truth could be warped and twisted by people's imaginations. The facts would be manipulated, and a completely different story would be created by their perverse minds. It was enough to fuel the community's anger, and the people began to use their own moral compass to condemn and judge me. I became a horrid wench. Every day, I became more and more detestable as the people continued to talk about me. The decrees of people became a strong wind and became a big storm of censure that swarmed over me. It was a storm that would engulf me. I could not see what was ahead of me.

I thought that Korean people were incredibly cruel while I was experiencing the aftermath of my in-law's death. I needed to separate myself from them as if I did not have a clue how much more savage they could be. Because of this issue, the oldest Korean church in Canada, the Korean United Church, was criticized by many Korean communities across Canada. Many people even gossiped about the late Reverand, Sang Cheol Lee, blaming and accusing him of his part in the transgression. They questioned his sermons and his moral compass for his part in having church members end up in such a horrific scandal. He endured through the defamation and slander while he made visits to us to comfort us and offer solace. We were too embarrassed to face him and apologized. Our church friends began to turn their backs on us saying they should not hang out with us anymore. I stopped going to the church that I poured love and devotion into after seeing how eager they all were to blame and condemn us.

We could bear the whole world pointing their fingers at us and saying whatever they wished as long as we had our church community's support. But when the people who gathered under God's love also began to point fingers and gossip behind our backs, it was an unbearable disappointment. Some suggested we leave Toronto and move to a quiet suburban area where few Koreans lived.

For a long time after that, I could not erase the memory of cold shoulders and blame I received from the Korean community and Korean church, so I attended a Canadian church instead. Only after a long time had passed and I grew numb to the pain, I returned to the church that blessed our in-laws and nephews with grace and started my Christian life in Canada. Perhaps it was my instinct to return to where I came from. After living through countless turmoil and pain, I learned about the power of love and forgiveness and decided to return to the church and to serve the church dutifully. The story of my brother-in-law and his wife shocked the Korean community and all of Canada and lasted as a traumatic story in the hearts and minds of many.

Fourteen years later, our oldest nephew followed his father's ways and ended his life. He was living a financially stable life where he did not have any economic worries, but I guess it was not enough to fill his heart. The world must have hurt him many times throughout his life with assumptions and tainted biases based on the scandal left by his parents. He was just a child who missed his parents greatly. He kept his distance from his only kin because he feared what the world would say and had to bear the weight of loneliness. The more I try to imagine the weight of his pain, the heavier my heart becomes as the feeling of pity and guilt overwhelms and consumes me slowly.

The youngest nephew was left alone so he decided to leave Ontario and go to a faraway province. He said life here was too painful for him and that he would not talk to anyone for a while in order to forget everything that happened here. He wished to leave in silence until peace was restored in his heart. I did not ask him where he was going and how long he was going for since I understood his feelings more than anyone else. We all decided to wait patiently until he reached out to us again. I am sure other members of the Korean community also had their share of cold and bitter feelings. It must have left my nephews feeling cold and empty. This case left only pain and sadness to all the parties and witnesses involved. Some days, I have futile thoughts of how different it may have been if we had held each other and supported one another through this pain and put effort into overcoming the trauma instead of looking for a person to blame.

These are futile thoughts because it is not based on my reality. I needed to expand my roots even further and sturdier to endure the powerful winds and the storm of sadness trying to envelope me. I needed to be a rock to stand up against the heavy winds with my frail body that could barely stand. I needed to be a mountain. I still had my precious children whom I needed to protect. They relied only on me, hiding from the gusts of storms in my arms. My husband shifted all the blame and resentment towards me, stood back, and watched as a bystander. He could not even handle his own pain and was always avoidant. Even if the storm rocked me, I could not be swept away. If I got swept away, our children would be sucked into the cruel snowstorm, and I could not let that happen. I did not care if fingers pointed in my direction. I just closed my eyes and wished all the negativity away and when I opened them, my life was completely shattered.

PART 3

My Story Lasts Within Me

Gathering Life...

The cruel times were slowly coming to an end. We closed our business and achieved freedom, or rather, I achieved freedom as I was not tied down to operating the storefront. Meanwhile, my husband studied Chinese medicine and shiatsu and opened a clinic in the basement of our new home. On the first floor, we had our shared family space such as a kitchen and living room; on the second floor, I had my personal space. Naturally, the basement became my husband's area, and as such, we separated our living space.

He and I were both traditional people. We did not expect anything from each other any longer since any feelings we had for one another dissipated into nothingness, but neither considered divorcing. I decided to live as is. Our relationship was tied by marriage, and I just needed to live on in a loveless marriage whether I liked it or not. If we needed to say or discuss something, we left notes on the fridge and maintained minimal communication with each other. Honestly, it was easier for me because I did not have to engage in conversation with him. I also found peace by doing what he required of me without any emotional connection and distanced myself from his verbal abuse.

My daughter entered university, and my two sons were high school students who grew up to be healthy and well. They did not cause any mischief, like most teenagers around their age, and they grew up to be my pride and joy. My husband would hang out with his friends after work, so my life was a lot more tranquil than before. I also spent my day getting involved in the Korean community and volunteering to improve our local area. I lived my life the way I chose to and pursued passions that went unattended instead of devoting myself entirely to my family and our livelihoods. I knew my husband was seeing other women, but I did not care. I was just thankful that he did not bother me and left me alone.

It must have been awkward for our grown children to understand. My daughter did not comprehend why her parents continued their marriage after seeing her father with another woman who introduced herself as a patient and ended up on the basement bed in pyjamas. It must have been difficult to watch us maintain this marriage because we had no love or faith in each other.

A call came in from our son's school one day; it seemed our oldest son was also having a difficult time accepting our arrangement although he never said anything. They let me know that his grades had dropped significantly and asked if there was any reason for it. I had never had a school call me for any kind of issues concerning our three children so I could sense that this was a serious matter, so I had a talk with my eldest son.

He confessed that every night he could hear his father talk to other women on his phone, and this angered him. He said that he wanted to see a counselor for therapy to help him process all the negative emotions he was feeling for his father. After some counseling and therapy, the counselor called me and carefully informed me that my son was having a difficult time handling his emotions after finding out about his father's affairs. They said this may be the reason why he could not focus on his schoolwork and asked if I was aware of my husband's indiscretions. My face warmed up from the embarrassment and I did not know what to say. On the one hand I wanted to admit his infidelity and on the other hand I was ashamed because I felt that my husband's indecent behaviour reflected on me. In the end, I told the truth and confessed that I knew about the affairs. It was a shameful and humiliating moment for me, but I realized after that I had no reason to be ashamed. I was not the one committing adultery. My family often went through small and big situations like this, and I just tried to overcome them stoically, while consoling and comforting my children so that I could alleviate as much of their emotional pain and suffering as I could.

My husband ran an acupuncture and shiatsu clinic in our basement, and for a more in-depth study he decided to go to study in China; he unfortunately did not let our family know of this decision. One late evening, our nephew came by to visit and say goodbye to his uncle since he was going to China. My husband had informed everyone around him of his plans to go to China except for me and our children. I could not understand how he could be so ruthless and insincere to our children. Once I heard that he was departing for China, I packed up his necessities and left them in his room. I waited for him in our kitchen early the next morning and prepared breakfast for him. I heard busy footsteps and frantic rustling from the basement hinting that he was getting ready to leave. I waited and waited while his breakfast turned cold but he did not come upstairs, so I went back up to my room on the second floor and, prayed for his safe trip before coming back down.

He was taking quite a long time to come up, so I opened the basement door to check on him. It was dark and quiet. I had a strange feeling and turned on the lights. He was not there. The clothes he wore lay on the ground and the travel attire I left spread out on the bed for him remained untouched. He had left through the back door while I was praying on the second floor without a word of farewell. 'Just what did I do wrong for him to leave without even saying goodbye?', I thought. Bidding adieu was just a decent thing to do, in my opinion. His vulgarity stunned me. His actions were uncivilized and crass, but I did not know what I was really upset about, but the heat burned my heart. I just stood there for a while, dumbfounded and wondered what all this was for. Why did I put up with his rudeness? I was better than that!

About a week before he left, we were returning home from his younger sister's house as she had recently immigrated to Canada and lived within driving distance. In the car ride back home, I mentioned to my husband that our eldest son wished to study at a prestigious university in America.

"Send him if you have the money," he replied coldly.

I was disappointed by his words and asked why he would not want his son to do well in life and succeed. But worse than that, I obviously made a grave mistake when I said,

"He's your son as well."

As soon as those words left my mouth, he embarked in a fit of rage and held on to the steering wheel with his left hand, and with his right punched the pit of my stomach. I could not breathe properly.

"I said you can send him if you have the money. You should be thankful that I lived with someone who is not innocent and pure. Other men would have kicked you out already," he said as he flew into a rage and the car shook with his anger.

I was scared for our lives that evening. As I sat in the car in fear, I thought, 'I need to put an end to our relationship today!' This I swore to myself and prayed that I had the strength to follow through with this promise to myself as soon as we arrived home, if we even made it home.

Once we thankfully reached our home, we went inside and the first thing he did was to pull out a beer from the refrigerator and handed me one as well. I threw the beer on the kitchen floor and yelled,

"If I'm a whore because I kissed someone else before marriage then what do you call yourself when you go around sleeping with other women while still married to me?"

I finally let all my feelings out and this spontaneous burst of emotion sparked a tirade within me. I began to throw anything within my reach: plates, glasses, and mugs. Nothing was safe if it was within my grasp. They all fell to the floor and shattered. There were so many shards on the ground that there was no space to walk without getting injured by a sharp piece of glass or porcelain.

My husband had never seen me behave so violently that it stunned him. He dragged me to our bedroom on the second floor and called a friend of mine to come over and calm me down. I refused to talk to her, and he became flustered because he did not know what to do with me. Up until that point, I was always calm and stoic in my demeanor. I was manageable then, but suddenly I became someone he did not recognize. I had changed into a different person right in front of his eyes. He had witnessed a transformation.

It is possible that the broken glass that covered the kitchen floor was the true picture of our marriage. I had endured so much pain and suffering until that moment when I finally could not take it anymore and everything exploded and flowed out of me and, I was finally able to breathe. When I went downstairs the next day, my husband mumbled that he cleaned up everything so our children would not see the mess I made. He avoided making eye contact with me and made an awkward facial expression to show his dissatisfaction. I later learned that he had already decided to go to China by this point, so I knew that my behaviour that night had nothing to do with his exodus.

Not long after he left for China, people around us began to ask me how he was doing there. I really could not answer their question since I honestly did not know how he was doing. There was no communication from him, but I supposed he was doing well. "Fine," I would say to anyone that asked about how he was doing. I received a letter soon after saying that he was doing well, but I still could not help being curious. My husband sent letters to everyone he knew to let them know how he was doing but did not send any news to me and our children. I thought I should not expect anything more from him, but I could not help feeling a bit bitter about it. It made me consider once more what it meant to be married and to have a family. My sister-in-law's words lingered in my mind, "No one, not even Koreans, live like you. You need to divorce him." She would often express her discontent about her brother. Even though he was her own flesh and blood, she could not understand his treatment of me. I thought maybe she was right and perhaps I was wrong in staying with him all this time. It was time lost that I would never get back.

There was a one-day seminar for women in London, Ontario, so I decided to attend. While I was there, the children unexpectedly called me saying that an intruder had come into our house, so the children called the police. I rushed back home and found my husband there; he had returned from China. Our children called the cops immediately when they heard some noise from the basement. My husband must have entered through the back door and was hiding in his bedroom because he could not face his children after leaving without saying goodbye. Our sons never thought that their father, who was supposed to be in China, returned home secretly.

Before he left for China, he met a Korean woman who had a family of her own. They had arranged to encounter each other in China but she did not meet him there and my husband returned to Canada temporarily to look for her. That is why he could not let us know that he was back home and tried to sneak in without alerting us of his return. I do not know how things ended up between my husband and that woman, but he left for China again soon afterward. After some time, he returned to Canada and asked for a divorce.

I was not at all surprised that he wanted to separate. I discovered that his reason for wanting to terminate our relationship was because he met a young Korean-Chinese woman when he arrived in Beijing and got her pregnant. He wanted to bring her to Canada and marry her, so he asked me for a quick divorce. He handed over full custody of our children without hesitation. It was not astonishing since he never showed love or affection towards them. We divided our assets as he wished and hired a lawyer to draw up a divorce settlement. I signed the documents he prepared one-sidedly. There was no need to hire another lawyer and contest the agreement as we had no objections or regrets about our marriage. We both wanted to move on in our separate ways.

He gave up a lot of our assets because I did not ask him for any financial help for our children after the divorce. According to the Canadian Family Law Act, married couples typically split their assets fifty-fifty, but he gave me more than half of our assets. He did not ask for my opinion, and I followed his decision as I only wanted to be free from this farse of a marriage and restore my peace of mind. Funny enough, this piqued many people's curiosity, and I received several phone calls asking how I could receive so much from our divorce. I also did not know what he was thinking when he divided our property. I can only assume that he must have offered me a more significant portion of our assets since I needed to bring up our children. Perhaps he thought that he could come back to me anytime and that I would accept him, and maybe this belief is what led him to settle for less. Nonetheless, we were finally divorced. Without this opportunity, we might have lived the rest of our lives without putting an end to our ridiculous marriage.

A Farewell Hard to Shake Off...

The marriage I never dared to end, even while experiencing all the hardships, wrapped up swiftly with just a couple of signatures. We may not have been divorced legally, but we lived mentally and physically separated for a long time, so it was nothing unusual. It was a farewell I had expected but the goodbye was still awkward.

I did not inform anyone around us or my family of our divorce. My mother never expected that one of her children would divorce. Telling her of this news would be like going against filial piety. It was my duty as a daughter to show courtesy and respect to my parents and in my culture, this meant staying married no matter what to uphold the family's virtue and reputation. So, I could not inform her of my unhappiness or even hint at my suffering. I was always careful to hide the pain in my voice whenever I called her.

My mother lost her husband during the war, and early in her marriage, the absence of a husband brought my mother great pain throughout our upbringing. There were no tremendous financial difficulties, but she was not free from society's prejudice against single mothers. She would be upset over how the world looked down on women who lived alone even when she was sick and bedridden. Although no one blamed her for losing a husband because of the war, there were some people who would rudely offend her greatly. For her, these insulting gazes were more upsetting to handle than the practical difficulties single mothers experienced. I did not think about divorcing my husband because these sentiments were rooted deep in my heart. That is why I had no courage to tell my mother about my divorce, and for five years after that, my family still did not know about our parting.

After my divorce, I was invited to attend the Peaceful Unification Advisory Council meetings in Korea and met my relatives there, who did not know about our divorce. My brother fussed about getting a whole set of new clothes from head to toe for his brother-in-law without knowing about my divorce. I could not say anything to him and tried to convince him to buy the clothes next time. There was also the hanbok my sister made for my husband; I had no choice but to bring that back to Canada with me. I am guessing it was because of our life experiences and mature age that my sister questioned several times if something was wrong with me. I tried to deny that anything had happened but instead of accepting my lies, she said, "No, you have a problem, something is strange. Is your husband having an affair?" She then said that women in our family are usually oblivious about these matters and suggested that we go to a sex education center in Yeouido. I said there was no need for that but on the other hand, I could not help feeling a bit bitter. I knew she thought that a man would only have an affair because women could not satisfy their husbands adequately, therefore a man's adultery was the woman's fault in her mind. I also wondered if people would forgive a woman for having an affair by blaming her husband for the wrong committed.

Back then, in Korea, people often used the expression that a woman is divorced from her husband. It did not matter who was at fault or who wanted to divorce. Women were always divorced by men. Korea still maintained the patriarchal family laws and family registry policies. The gender equality promised by the constitution was structurally unfavourable to women in the civil laws. Some laws restricted and violated women's rights to divorce or re-marry. Until the end of the 1990s, there was a self-deprecating joke amongst people who worked to improve the family laws that women had the right to be divorced but not the right to divorce. People must have felt these limits and discriminations in their daily lives to use such expressions, even though most people did not know the laws well enough or even imagined that a law was created to discriminate systemically. These discriminations are naturally absorbed into people's daily language, and people use such expressions daily without realizing it. Thus, using the expression that a man divorced a woman was not awkward in those days.

The bias and discrimination related to divorce were not much different in the Korean immigrant community. In some areas, it was worse. In Canada, it seemed that in most divorce cases women were filing for divorce. So, if a man filed for divorce first, Korean people would typically gossip about how weird the wife must be for a man to file for divorce first and start talking negatively about someone that they had never met.

Per Korean values, it was assumed of women to follow her husband's beck and call so there was no reason for a man to divorce his wife in any case if she was dutiful. These old-fashioned Korean values did not change much after moving to Canada. Canadian women seemed less concerned with the prejudices of being a divorcee than Koreans so they did not just sit through an unhappy marriage and would end it. But most Koreans believed baseless words without fact-checking much of what they heard and were especially critical of cases where a man filed for divorce first.

That is one of the reasons I was not eager to inform the people around me of my divorce. They would have slandered me as well and assumed that my difficult personality caused the disparage for our family. It would not have mattered to them that he wanted to divorce me so that he could bring his new wife to Canada legally. The truth did not matter as they would belittle and criticize me, nonetheless. I did not want that stigma placed upon me and just hoped everything would pass as if nothing had happened.

My assumptions were not wrong. As soon as people found out about our divorce, they assumed that I was at fault for the divorce and slandered me greatly. I was called all kinds of unfavourable names and stories were made up about what an awful wife I had been to him. Eventually, people realized what happened when he returned to Toronto with a new wife and daughter, yet they came up with a different reason to continue to blame me. Words circulated saying I was a woman who counted flies on the ceiling while making love, and they commented on my husband's patience and tolerance for me saying what man would love a woman who is not good enough in the bedroom but a very considerate and honourable man.

For people who thought other people's family drama was entertainment, the real reason for divorce did not matter to them. It seemed like people were focused on slighting me and the truth never mattered in the first place. They just wanted a good story to tell until another good story came along. All I did was wait for them to get tired of telling the same story. I knew they would eventually, that is why I was not bothered by all the gossip.

There was no difference in our lives before and after the divorce since our lifestyle did not change much other than the fact that we lived in separate abodes. He was with other women outside the house, as per usual, and I was at home caring for our children alone. My life remained the same as if nothing changed. If it was this easy to end it all, what was I doing all this time? Why had I not done this earlier? The answer was simple. I was concerned about what people would say and what people thought about me. Now that our divorce had become reality, the experience was not as bad as I thought it was going to be. I was strong and I could handle the peering gazes and the whispers behind my back. They could judge me if they wanted as I knew that no one was free from sin, and they had no business casting stones my way.

Hard Goodbyes...

Our goodbye was as difficult as shaking off flakes of dry leaf stuck to a knit sweater. He returned with another woman and their daughter but was still thinking of me as if I were his possession to do as he pleased. Whenever he needed something and was unsatisfied with something, he reached out for my help as if it were the normal thing to do. I am unsure if it was out of habit or if it was because I did not have any feelings towards him since we were separated for so long, but I did not refrain from helping him settle in with his wife. They did not have basic household items, so I gave them a car, clothes, and other items. These were unnecessary things for me, so I just wanted to get rid of them.

My daughter hated seeing me help him.

"Are you still waiting for Dad?" she asked, disgusted by my apparent subservience to him.

"No, I needed to organize our stuff and just sent what we didn't need to the people who needed it." I replied, matter-of-factly.

"Mom, you are still holding on to Dad's sleeves, not letting him go," she accused.

"Your father and I worked together to buy all these things. We are going to use it. Should I give it to a stranger or give it to your dad, who needs it right now?" I wanted to show her I had no hard feelings toward him.

She thought that her father did not have any right to request anything and did not deserve my help, and she would hate to see me helping him. She shook her head even when I explained that I was only sending things I did not need anymore.

One day I received a call from him saying that his daughter had a high fever but could not go to the hospital because she did not have healthcare insurance. I remember the first time I arrived in Canada with my daughter. Back then, he would just watch our daughter roll around from the pain of a high fever and give the excuse that he did not have insurance yet. Eventually, I called a taxi and took our daughter to the hospital by myself. I had a flashback to this moment and knew he would not do anything for his sick child, yet he could not turn away from helping his new wife and their daughter. I contacted different people to treat the sick child first. The vaccine area on the child's arm was infected and they had to drain a cup full of pus from the infected area. Thanks to these helpful people, her young life was saved, and she slept soundly and peacefully that night. I did not know if I was just used to enduring and offering help or if I was a fool like my daughter had said. It was just that he needed help, and I helped him because I could.

I had already given up on him and did not blame him anymore. I could not understand the pain and betrayal that our children experienced during the years of his absence. No matter how deep my love was for them, a father's love was not something I could replace. They did not have the courage to express their longing for fatherly love in front of me because they knew how much I loved and cared for them.

I felt how difficult it was for them to acknowledge their father, who had never given them any love while growing up, disappeared without a word, only to suddenly show up with a different family without any explanations. I overlooked the fact that these actions would have hurt our children even if they were used to their father behaving in such a manner. I did not think to console them and help them work through their turbulent emotions. No, perhaps, because I was too complacent, I thought that I did not have to address any of this ugliness. As a mother, I believed I had taught my children to be strong and I did not think they needed any embraces or long discussions about our family matters. Thinking back on it now, I realize that both their father and I were unconcerned about the separation our children also had to experience. A part of me believed that since they had always endured well and grew up to be kind souls no matter how difficult our circumstances were, I trusted that they would get over this sudden split as well. Now, my heart and mind feel sorry for not caring about their emotional pain back then.

One day, I asked my youngest son, who was now an adult, if he missed his father. Since their last farewell, he had not contacted him even once, so it was nothing new, but I still worried that our youngest missed his father since he was the most affectionate with him. He responded as if it was no matter to him.

"Mom, you can only miss something you had before. How could I miss dad when he was not even there when I was growing up." He said, wisely.

I felt ashamed by his words. I held on to our marriage thinking that an illusion of a mother and father living under the same roof would benefit our children. How wrong I was! They had already let go of their father long ago.

Throughout our time together my husband would threaten me if I ever mentioned divorce. He would say that with just a couple of thousands of dollars, he could hire someone to kill me. He then stopped with his menacing ultimatums. But he had never let go of me even while not loving me, and I do not know for what reason, but he stayed with me just like that. So, did I. We were bound to each other by forces that even we could not explain. But finally, we could let go. The farewell between us was also a farewell to all the problematic and suffocating times.

After Crying for a While ...

Time went by inevitably. The world continued to go on as usual regardless of what I was going through. The sun continued to rise and set regardless of whether I felt miserable or happy. In life, I know one thing is true: You will eventually feel hungry, and sleep will come when you become tired after so many days that you feel like you cannot laugh. Finally, a day will come when you laugh out loud. Things that go on unavoidably have the power to heal our wounds and numb our pain. My day-to-day life was also like that. My pain faded with the passing of time and the warmth of love I received as I interacted with people and thought about how to live, help one another, and give a hand to those who need it. More than anything else, my three children all grew up to be my pride and joy, and the fact that they were all living their own lives comforted me greatly.

Unlike my two sons, my daughter always pitied my lifestyle. As the oldest child, she had the misfortune to witness her parent's relationship from a young age and had to act as a mother for our two sons when I was out busy working to support our family. If there was something to discuss, the boys would look for their sister before they approached me. Since I was usually busy with big and small issues at the store and at home, their sister usually pampered them. I felt that our youngest could not come to me but rather talked to his sister when he had a stomach-ache. I pitied my daughter who could not help but shout, "Am I your mother?"

The emptiness I could feel no matter how hard I tried to fill the void was palpable. They relied on each other.

At school, my daughter was educated in the Canadian way, and at home, she witnessed her parents have a traditional Korean relationship. She pitied the way I lived as a wife as she grew up. At the same time, she found it difficult to understand why I would not get out of such an inhuman and unfair marriage. I noticed she was seeing me from a different perspective than my boys because she was also a woman. My daughter did not understand why I was passively accepting everything and did not know what to do except feel upset and worried at the same time over my situation.

I also did not have any way of explaining to her why I was living this way in a logical manner. I learned that once you are married, you must stay with your husband no matter the circumstances. A wife had to tolerate everything no matter what their husband did. How can I reasonably explain that I was living just for living's sake? My mother had said that the husband is the sky, and the wife is the earth, and her words dominated my heart and mind all my life, and I thought it was natural to obey my husband as a wife. When I could not submit entirely to my husband's unjust words or actions, I at least tried to look as if I regretted not being able to obey completely. I could not answer honestly and earnestly when my daughter asked why I married her father. I had forgotten why I fell in love with him in the first place.

I had never thought about why one needed to marry, so I did not know why I married. Back then, one married when it was time to do so. Just like how summer comes after spring, people married when they were old enough to marry. Of course, I am sure some people married because they loved one another, but most married when it was time to do so and began to love each other since they were married. It is not like everyone falls in love around the same age, but we tied marriage to people's age instead of tying love with marriage, having children together, and creating a family. After exchanging their marriage vows, couples would try to start a loving relationship, and even if they failed, they continued to live together since they were already married. People needed to be more ashamed of not marrying when they were old enough instead of marrying a person they did not love. Couples feared freeing each other from unhappy marriages rather than living miserably together while hating each other. People's thoughts about love, marriage, and divorce differ based on generation or culture. I did not know how to explain the love affairs of my generation to my children, who live in a completely different time and culture.

I did not know how to make my children understand things that did not make sense and should not have taken place according to them. My daughter and I must have had a gap in understanding because we were two women with different experiences. The views of men and women have changed significantly since my time. The gender roles and values of my daughter's world differed considerably from my generation's. I knew things had changed and people's thinking was much different now, but no one was telling us exactly how things had changed. I did not have a way of explaining to my daughter since I also did not know how and in what form our values and notions differed.

My daughter could not just criticize me for my impracticality, but she also did not have the confidence or the courage to continue seeing her mother live on like that. After graduating from McGill, she went off on a trip to Africa with her university boyfriend. I could not see her, let alone exchange a word with her for a year at least. The credit card statements delivered every now and then were the only confirmation I had that she was alive in Africa.

From the first moment she came to me, my daughter was the joy of my life. I waited for her with complete happiness. I waited for her without any worry, and she was my alter ego. She was a child who helped me feel the joy of being a mother for the first time. I hid my pain from them all the time because I worried it would be too difficult for my children to see. I wanted our children to live within our safe fence and I was able to endure all that suffering and unfairness for them. But these efforts had brought my daughter great pain. My unexplainable desperation and suffering must have been too painful to witness. After completing a year-long trip in Africa, she immediately went to Bristol University in the UK to start her master's degree with her boyfriend.

During their master's program, they planned to get married and my soon-to-be son-in-law's parents invited me to their cottage in Malaga, Spain. My son-in-law's parents were from a prestigious Italian family, and I was with them for the Easter holiday season. It was a precious time for me as I finally got to see my daughter and spend time with her for two weeks, which was not too long. I could stay in a separate condo with my daughter thanks to my son-in-law's affluence. After a long time, I finally got to see my daughter face-to-face. My emotions got the better of me and I almost cried.

Malaga was full of warm sunshine all day long. The blue ocean left me in awe that such colours truly exist, and the wind always carried the fragrance of flowers. Our condo had a picture-perfect view of the sandy beach and the big blue ocean. You could reach the shore within just a few steps on the fine sandy beach. Malaga in April was a fairytale-like place with white buildings and a vast open sea. There were many dark-skinned and shorter people compared to northern Spain because, for eight hundred years, it was under the influence of the Moorish people of North Africa.

My soon-to-be in-laws welcomed me with bright smiles full of energy. Thanks to their warm welcome, there was no time to be uneasy when we first met. Instead, there was some unease between me and my daughter. My daughter's future mother-in-law, Anne, was born and raised in Canada. She studied English at Queens University and met her husband while working as a teacher. Her husband was completing his master's at Western University as an international student. The two married and began their life together in Italy.

DANDELION OF THAT WINTER

She suggested exploring the Malaga area with me so we could have our own mini vacation. It was unexpected, but I did not oppose it, and we set off on a three-day trip together.

I am unsure if it was the power of beautiful sceneries that opened my heart or her warmth toward me waking up my dormant emotions, but soon she and I acted like old friends. We explored the beautiful sights in Sevilla and Granada and looked around in Picasso's home. After that, we went to a mystical underground cave that must have formed over thousands of years. Anne and I laughed like teenage girls as we shared our life stories and learned about the differences in our cultures and lifestyles. We found similarities that surpassed the differences, and I had not felt at peace like that in a long time.

The first two nights we stayed in the same hotel room. We talked and listened to each other about the life we have lived. The most correct way to describe that time would be that we genuinely shared our hearts and souls. She wished to know about my life. Anne said that when my daughter visited their home for the first time and was asked about her father, she cried silently. After crying for a while, my daughter explained that she could not help but cry when she found out that a fatherly figure could be so warm and loving, and she thought of me and wondered why I had lived in such a foolish way.

I could not wait any more when I heard Anne had invited me there to understand my daughter's pain and to help heal her wounds. I could not sit in my armour of pride, and I needed to take it off immediately. Words started to pour out of my mouth with no order. All this time, I had lived hating myself for not standing up for myself. I had never said a word to anyone around me about what a difficult time it was having to protect my pride without shedding a single tear. There was no way I could tell the truth to the people around me who thought I was a lucky woman, nor did I want to. I only smiled on the outside and cried on the inside. I was locked up in the darkness that I could not share or expose to anyone. There were only nights full of darkness in my heart.

Maybe I needed someone to just hear me out for a long time. On that day, Anne became the person who could listen to my story with no judgment on whether I was right or wrong and just listened solemnly. She offered her shoulder for me to cry on, and I cried, letting out all my sadness and hardships. I finally had a friend who could listen to my feelings, something even my closest family or kin could not understand. I told her how and why I lived like I did without hesitation or fear. I was not afraid of her judgment and did not fear my words being twisted and traveling to other people. That night, we talked about a woman who endured everything through foolish bravery, mighty grit, and strong determination for a long time.

I met my daughter again after returning from the trip. We were too busy with everyday life and did not have time of our own so we could not tend to the hurt we endured even though we were aware of it. So much time had passed, and I did not know what to do in front of her resentment, although I knew she did not resent me.

"Mom, what did you like about Dad for you to live with him? Why did you live the way you lived? Do you remember when I asked you to run away in grade five? Why did you live so foolishly?" She began to pour out the words she had bottled up for a long time.

I remember when she was barely ten and she suddenly asked me if I had any money saved. I looked back, confused, and she replied, "Mom, let's start saving money from now on and run away from Dad together." My heart ripped apart thinking how painful it must have been for her to remember that time even to this day.

I cried and cried and silently screamed, 'I lived that way because of the three of you. I believed he could become a good father someday if I just endured and waited patiently.' 'Yes, I also wanted to run away. I wanted to run away a hundred, no, a thousand times.' I remembered my mother-in-law as I swallowed these words. My mother-in-law came to stay in Canada for a while and witnessed how her son treated me, and said, "You are living well without running away. I didn't give birth to a son like that. If that was my husband, I would have run away more than ten times." She returned to Korea before I gave birth to our youngest. All I wanted to do was provide my children with a happy and complete family. I felt perplexed that I refused to believe the reality that everyone saw and stubbornly held on to a façade.

Anne watched my daughter and I talk, and afterward, she set off on a journey with my daughter alone. She volunteered to be my representative while spending some time face-to-face with my daughter. Although my daughter was my flesh and bone, the generational and cultural differences that impacted our thoughts and opinions were already far too big of a caveat between her and me to communicate easily. I believed Anne would touch her heart just like she did mine, so I waited patiently and calmly by the ocean.

After spending the night with Anne, my daughter returned. I could feel her body shaking as she hugged me tightly and cried. I could feel her warmth and I cried endlessly as well. Anne told my daughter about her experience immigrating to Italy from Canada, the hardships that followed, the language barrier, cultural differences, and the difficulties of married life. She explained that she could endure the tough times thanks to her loving husband, and although I did not have a loving husband, it was thanks to my children that I could live on through the difficulties. Anne explained to my daughter that I am not stupid or lacking sense; it was just that for me, my children were more precious than my own life, so I sacrificed my life to protect my family and my children's lives. Anne explained to my daughter that it may not fit her generation's standards, but in our generation, that was how we protected the things and people we cared for, and that her mother wanted to protect her children even if it meant throwing herself away. My daughter cried and cried after Anne explained this to her.

My daughter held on to me for a long time, crying, "Mom, I'm sorry. I'm sorry I was mean to you and didn't understand you."

I was thankful that she understood me and felt sorry, although it pained me. I felt sorry because she had me as a mother, she experienced heartbreaks she would not have needed to experience, and I felt remorseful that I did not give more love and affection to her. I could not keep my head up at the thought of not being able to care for them enough because I was too busy with our day-to-day lives when I knew they grew up without their father's love. For a long time, she assumed the position of a substitute mother to her younger siblings and played the role of a father. I detested myself thinking about it.

That's how we set off on our journey to heal each other's wounds. Suddenly, she had grown to be a mature adult who tried to understand and share her mother's life and pain. I was thankful for that. She attempted to take my suffering upon herself despite not quite understanding why and how but through her efforts, I felt her love and it brought me immense happiness.

"Mom, if there is a field of study you didn't get to complete, you should finish it. To attend a university, you need a TOEFL score, so you should start English school first. And if you want to do your master's or doctorate after university, do it. I will cheer you on," she said, encouragingly.

Since she knew how much I loved to study, she must have considered how I could continue my education and urged me that it was not too late to continue and offered to support me any way she could.

After a brief pause, she slowly said, "And Mom, promise me one thing. Promise me that you will get some counseling to relieve the pain and sadness deep in your heart so you can live your life happily after. And please turn your story into writing, not just for you, but for all of us as well."

I guess she could see it. She could see my painful past that I threw somewhere far away within my mind, and it was concealed somewhere in there. She could see the bruises and lumps that her father caused and that had held me back from moving forward. She told me to find my past self and tend to my old cuts and wounds. I needed to look back on different parts of me through different times and have a moment to console and comfort myself. Without doing this, I could not move forward. If I allow the sweet rain to fall on my barren emotional garden, the warmth will sprout, and one day, colourful emotions will bloom again.

I tried to face my old self and turn those hard times into writing as per my daughter's advice, but I could not start properly for a long time after that. Since I could not begin my memoir, I could not wrap it up. The pain overwhelmed my body and mind whenever I looked back on my past traumas, and the weight of sadness suffocated me. I started writing many times but was never able to finish it. I realized I needed time to collect myself first and strengthen myself. I needed to find myself and the self I left behind to face myself with courage during the tough process of remembering some of my most dreadful memories.

Pain, happiness, and sadness were all a part of my life. It was time to claim my inner strength that had been supressed for years and proceed with my life. Malaga's blue sky and ocean met under the bright sun and shone brightly. It was magnificent. It was shining, and it was warm. The fresh smell of the ocean traveled with the wind and tickled my heart. The beauty of it all made my slumbering heart awaken and beat again. I realized that this was a fresh start. My entire being including my vanquished soul was reviving and arousing within me again. It was like a re-birth. I could finally be me again.

Missing Myself...

I needed to bring myself out of my reclusive and dark world. I set off on an impromptu adventure without much thought. I left for Europe with some of my friends. I hoped to let go of what bothered me and find time to build a new life. I looked around at the beautiful, shining world that was inviting me in, and befriended several kind and considerate people. I sought people with sympathetic souls to soothe my heart and build myself up. I let go of the countless treacheries I experienced in my past relationship and grounded my heart to not be swayed by betrayals of love. I spent a lot of time writing to shake the pain out of me. I left myself behind, and I found myself again. I discovered myself, a woman who had lived as if she did not exist during her time with her husband, and I gave myself a voice by writing. My composition was a confession to myself, not to anyone else. It was a tiring but necessary time. But through writing, I was able to find myself and return home.

The first thing I wanted to do as a new-found person was to study. I first signed up for English school per my daughter's advice but could not put my heart into it. It was challenging to focus on anything while my mind was racing with thoughts of all that I wanted to accomplish. Everything began to feel useless because there was so much I wanted to do but did not know where to start. I did not understand why I struggled to live without clear answers. There were moments when I did not know how I wanted to live. It was like I was all burnt out when I had not even started

DANDELION OF THAT WINTER

living my life. Spending time moping around felt wasteful. I knew that I had the luxury of autonomy over my own person, but I feared that the spring of positivity had dried out within me. I did not know what to do with this unexpected feeling and felt troubled.

I set foot towards the world recklessly. Sure, I was hurt by people and was tired of the cruelness some individuals exhibited towards me, but my heart knew that I needed to be around people to heal, and that is how I found answers. I did not have a plan and merely did what I could and needed to do in this world. Through these ambiguous times, I was able to learn from those around me what type of person I was and how bright and energetic I used to be. I found my old self, whom I missed very dearly, by actively participating and volunteering in the Korean community. It was not what I had intended, but I found my forgotten self by putting myself to good use where humankind needed me. I was able to bring myself up by working hard to achieve something better for the people around me. Without realizing it, I could slowly return to my old self by offering myself to those who needed my help. Witnessing their success, was very justifying and rewarding for me and this assisted me in getting me out of my slump.

It is because of this reason that the Korean Canadian Women's Association is an incredibly cherished connection for me. The Korean Canadian Women's Association was established in 1985. They aimed to help the Korean immigrant community have a healthy and happy life in Canada. They had programs to raise awareness about health, settlement, accounting, employment, leisure, and family services to help the lives of the Korean community.

Korean immigrant families experienced many hardships adjusting to the fast-changing society and cultural differences. There had been conversations about how to effectively help Korean families and the need for an organization that could serve as the main pillar of this support system. My brother-in-law's tragic incident must have been the catalyst because the

Korean Canadian Women's Association was founded after rushing to be created in July, two months after the traumatic event. The murder-suicide shocked the nation and heightened the interest in the immigrant community as well as their role and responsibility within the nation. The Korean Canadian Women's Association intended to provide a wide variety of information and services needed in the immigrant community. I mainly took a liking to them not only because they were helping improve the quality of life for Korean immigrants but also to help represent women and their growth as meaningful individuals in a society where women were still considered a minority.

I firmly believe that if more women can be responsible for themselves instead of relying on others, our society can be healthier, and everyone could be happier. As much as women were forced to live dependent lives, many men could not be free from unwanted responsibility and obligation. Once there is an enlightened view of women's roles in society, we can reconsider the roles of men. That way, women and men can build their own lives with their own choices without the pressure of social gender roles. I chose to be with the Korean Canadian Women's Association to distinguish men and women in a healthy and non-discriminating manner.

Looking back on my marriage with my husband, I often wonder if I was the only victim in that relationship. I question if he was suffering from the pressure of society and the expectation of a man's role. It may have forced him to behave in a certain way. Perhaps he was unhappy with the way his life turned out, and the only way to exist was to vent those pent-up feelings towards me because I was closest to him and also weakest around him. Possibly, he lost his warm feelings and human innocence trying to hold the unbearable weight and expectation of being the 'man of the house.' Seeing how he failed to have shown fatherly love for his children, I do not think my guesses are too far off, but I do not want to make excuses for him.

DANDELION OF THAT WINTER

He probably did not want to live an ordinary life and take responsibility for his family, as was expected as 'a man.' Perhaps he did not have the courage to tell the world he did not wish to undertake this prominent and important task. I wonder how different his pain is compared to my own, when I had endured unhappy times because I feared society's view of divorced women. It was probably because of this societal pressure (of providing for one's family) that caused his stress. He could not complain about this responsibility or else face conviction from his peers, so his complaints went muffled, and so he had to put on a façade of an ordinary family man in public. This may be why his contradicting personality felt sad to me at times.

I was the chairman of the women's association twice, from 1992 to 1994, and hosted many events. Among them, my most memorable event was the 1992 seminar and memorial worship hosted for Military comfort women. Comfort women were women that were forced into sexual slavery by the imperial Japanese army in its occupied territories during World War II. Stories of comfort women were deemed personal claims and were mostly denied until August 1991, when Asahi News of Japan released an article about it to tell the whole world that these atrocities did in fact occur. The Japanese reporter Uemura Takeshi had always been interested in human rights issues, and his article helped bring awareness about the plight of comfort women during the war. The Korean Women's Association in Canada decided to hold the seminar as we thought of this issue as an extension of human rights and women's rights. We felt it was our duty to discuss these issues.

We banded with other organizations within Toronto to raise awareness about comfort women in the international platform. We also invited one of the victims of the wartimes, Geum Joo Hwan, and listened to her vivid tale of what happened to her. We wrote petitions to send to the UN, wrote reports about the surviving comfort women, and gathered donations to help their lives even if by a bit. The efforts of the women's association soon brought lots of sympathy from many communities. It was also written in the Canadian daily newspapers, and it helped tell the world about the crisis faced by comfort women. The photo gallery exhibition that took place at the Metro Toronto Library, 'Military Sexual Slave Photo Exhibition,' garnered a lot of attention and rang the hearts of many community members. Various Korean churches across Canada, such as the Korean United Church, Korean Presbyterian Church, and Korean Anglican Church, donated funds and showed interest in the cause.

The surviving elderly women had been drafted to war in their youth and were victims of the war. Their human rights were abused under the Japanese ruling government. They hid from the world after the war ended for a long time, not only because of the Korean government's neglect but also because of the moral virtue that the nation had and were ashamed of them. Women were always compelled to be chaste physically, and such obligation gave people justification to blame these victims of war for losing their virtue. Because of these ideals and uptight morality, countless women from China, Korea, and other countries that Japan occupied during the war had to undergo the pain of silence and the memories of their suffering without being able to talk to anyone and share their dreadful experiences.

These helpless victims were stuck in the social trap that the offenders placed upon them and could not even plea for help. They endured for a long time in silence without being able to say a word. The victims were hiding the crimes of their oppressors and the physical and mental damages they experienced. Offenders were probably scrambling to hide their wrongdoings, and in the process of hiding, they must have committed more crimes against humanity. In the end, they must have given themselves some justification that their way was necessary and faultless. The offenders may have become more evil and wicked over time as they tried to argue that their wrongs were right, even though they knew they were wrong. The transgressors were hiding their guilt and shame behind society's shield and shifted the blame and responsibility to the victims.

Through workshops that focused on comfort women and women who were drafted to war, we focused on the lives of these victims, and I became more aware of the problems that gender stereotypes or gender discrimination within our society can bring. I also realized that my past days were not completely unrelated to these stereotypes. In the past, whenever my husband acted unfairly, I would glide over it by thinking, 'This is how men are. Because he is a man, he can.' The stereotypes I had had allowed me to justify his actions, and perhaps my husband did not realize that his actions were wrong because of these stereotypes. Of course, his actions were wrong, but they were accepted societally, so there was not much objection that could take place. Despite the social norms, my heart could not accept these actions wholeheartedly, so without realizing, a wall was erected between my husband and I. One will need to investigate how these discriminating gender stereotypes can build many invisible walls in countless households.

Violence cannot be justified under any circumstances. No one has the right to abuse another or treat them however they wish. It is a crime that cannot be justified under social norms or standards. This conviction in me makes it difficult for me to forgive my husband's actions.

While organizing the seminar on military sex slaves, we contemplated the direction that the Korean Canadian Women's Association must take going forward. In the process of it, we found a solution. A more educated understanding of women's rights and their role within a family environment was most important. Once the awareness of women's roles are improved, there can be forgiveness and coexistence, allowing both men and women to live free from gender stereotypes. The Korean Canadian Women's Association existed to break the barrier between men and women set by gender stereotypes, and people also gathered to take on the responsibility of spreading Korean culture and history to the rest of the world.

There were various attempts to understand women's insights and to straighten the role of women in both society and in the household. Thanks to these efforts, the provincial government funded the association to host a National Women's Conference at the Palm Plaza Hotel for two nights and three days. The conference invited about one hundred female professionals who were mostly East Asian, like Korean and Japanese. There was also a discussion about racial discrimination under the theme of 'women in transition.' We also discussed the difficulties of the language barrier and accepting a new culture from many different points of view. Thanks to this event, Toronto's recognition of the Korean Canadian Women's Association was greater.

The workshop looked closely at the reality of Canada's racial discrimination. It brought lots of attention from people to be more aware of the discrimination that exists structurally and systemically within our society. People also shared their experiences with discrimination and racism in their daily lives. Although I do not often feel discriminated against daily, I also experienced an absurd situation in France while on vacation. I was at my hotel having breakfast, and a Caucasian woman walked up to me and spat on my food with no explanation. She seemed displeased that an Asian woman was having breakfast in the same space as her in a nice hotel. I was in disbelief.

For the most part, I believe that racism is the problem of those individuals who actively discriminate. Although my belief has not changed much, I learned that discrimination can occur institutionally and structurally. In a country like Canada, where many different cultures coexist, understanding and showing respect is needed from one culture to another for us all to live harmoniously. I hope that through educating ourselves about different cultures, we will fertilize our society to adjust to differences more positively.

DANDELION OF THAT WINTER

In Canada, there are a lot of immigrants from North Korea. Many of them chose to come to Canada after experiencing discrimination and isolation from Korea. Although they were of the same ethnic background, the cultural differences caused a rift. The effort to understand another person is inevitably understanding our own thought processes that can cause dissonance with others. This is the starting point for my efforts to live harmoniously with others. We think we are learning about different cultures and races, but really, we are learning about ourselves in the process. We learn about ourselves as much as we learn about others to slowly understand one another more closely.

When I was living in Ottawa, a South Asian neighbour living on the first floor of our apartment building taped a court decree on their front door. Our neighbourhood was considerably affluent, and the residents of that apartment complex complained that the South Asian neighbour was making curry too often, which eventually led to a court dispute asking for the South Asian neighbours to move out of the apartment. The court sided with the South Asian neighbour's love for curry, stating that if no illegal ingredients are involved, then one has the right to cook whichever dish they desire. I was also not the biggest supporter of strong curry and spicy smells, but I thought that my dislike was not a reason for me to violate their rights. If I do not know something or cannot understand, then that is my problem, and it does not necessarily mean it is wrong; this is especially the case when various cultures coexist in the same space. The curry incident helped me understand this.

One time, when my husband was returning home from working at the gas station all day, one of the neighbours stopped him from entering the building. He told the neighbour this was his home, but they did not let him pass. Only after the building manager came by to confirm that my husband lived in the building could he return home. Since he was a visible minority and had shabby clothes, he became the target of people who judged others based on looks. It was a good example showcasing the unfair treatment one can receive based on stereotypes and prejudice.

Perhaps an effort to learn about differences based on race, gender, culture, and generation diminishes discrimination and is the best way to exist together harmoniously. Human beings are all different, even if they are of the same culture, race, or sexuality. It is possible that discriminating against other races and cultures inevitably removes all our patience towards one another. This is why understanding differences in a mature and sensible manner and learning how to express respect and justness for one another is crucial in our society.

Among many different departments in the Korean Canadian Women's Association, the women who married internationally and single mother groups had a special place in my heart. It is rare to find marriages where there is not much difficulty, and it is always smooth sailing. International couples often have additional problems than other married couples because of having to overcome cultural and language differences. The Korean Canadian Women's Association wished to mentor these women and share the wisdom gained from experiencing immigrant life. We offered them solutions to fix problems arising from language and cultural barriers, and when women faced problems, they could not resolve alone, we offered our help as well.

In transnational marriages, Korean women often faced problems arising from different expectations of the role of women in a home. For Korean women, it was a typical expectation to stay at home after marriage, overlook the accounts of the house and manage the household. Men who were born and raised in Canada, distinguished the difference between communal expenses and individual assets, even in marriage. I witnessed problems among these transnational couples where a Korean wife asked her Canadian husband for a monthly income. The husband found it difficult to understand why his Korean wife was asking for his pay stub, and the Korean wife understood his rejection as distrust. Another common problem was that some husbands would insinuate that their stay-at-home wife was not working hard enough, as it seemed that they were just at home hanging around all day, not doing anything constructive. Although both parties understood that they were from different cultures, there was no guideline to understand these perceived differences, and often, emotions and differences deepened, and marriages turned volatile.

The language barrier probably also widened the drift between a husband and wife. The Korean Canadian Women's Association contemplated how to make these couples understand the small but vast differences among us and how to resolve the heightened tension within families wisely. I also opened my eyes while working with them. I could see how tall of a wall these small differences could pile together and form. In the end, culture is an expression of one's living environment and way of thinking. I thought that maybe my husband and I overlooked our differences that could naturally exist because we were fooled by the fact that we are from the same country and spoke the same tongue.

Some say that Canada is better than Korea, but even in Canada, domestic violence laws and policies were not entrenched in society until the 1990s. Only in the late 1970s did the government publicly announce that violence within domestic settings is considered a crime. The official domestic violence call hotline was developed in the 1980s for people to report domestic abuse. It took ten years for the government to enact the laws related to domestic abuse and made them widely known. It took ten years for people to recognize the need for these laws and enact them, so we can only imagine how long it must have taken people to recognize these laws and actively engrain them into their daily lives.

Some Korean women at the time could not help but be a weaker party in marriage regarding financial means and other factors that made them be the dependant party in the relationship. Because of this, they tended to be victims of domestic abuse. Their children were also inescapably exposed to domestic abuse in a household like that. The Korean Canadian Women's Association attempted to increase understanding and teach preventative measures to raise awareness about female abuse in the Korean community through the Korean Immigrant Family Problem Seminars. I also spoke at one of the seminars and wrote columns about abuse that women fell victim to in domestic settings and I put forth ideas to change the notion about this subject. Understanding the issues were the starting point for solving their problems. Generally, issues among married couples or family were resolved once people gathered and talked calmly about all their problems and were able to heal through sharing experiences.

In most Korean families, domestic problems did not necessarily arise from the husband's or the wife's personality. Often, it was the deeply ingrained cultural customs and practices that brought problems to these couples. Numerous issues arose from being unable to have fluid conversations with each other and with their children because this was not ordinarily practised in the Korean culture. When stressed from many different aspects of life, it was hard to expect one to resolve problems with their families, so our association tried to offer them tools to resolve their dilemmas. We had seminars, workshops, and other talks planned for families going through traumatic times to offer them a helping hand institutionally so they can understand the root cause of their problems adequately and find ways to resolve their issues in a shielded and comfortable environment and give them the tools to prevent similar situations in the future.

I knew from my experience that these people were in dire need of emotional help. My objective was to tend to their psychological wounds. Most importantly, I could refrain from judging or criticizing how they lived because I had been in their position. I knew how hurtful critical words could sometimes be, so I would do nothing more than offer help and directions to resolve their issues. No one in this world lives miserably because they wish to live miserably. They do not choose to live these difficult lives. I understood that most problems people faced were because they could not analyze the root cause of the problem and did not know how to resolve their issues with the limited resources available to them.

I comforted myself by realizing that I was not alone in these painful experiences. Instead of blaming myself for living the way I had lived in the past, I absorbed myself in these people's experiences to comfort them as well. With love, I faced their problems together with them, and I was also able to face my past self, whom I had thought was ignorant and pathetic and learned to love myself in the end. I found my alter ego hiding from the world because I was scared, although I knew I had done no wrong, so I encouraged myself to face the world's animosity.

I often think that if we had not provided the resources for these families back then, how different their lives may have been. I felt some regret because if my family had these resources back then, my children, my husband and I could all love each other more and live happily together instead of ending up in divorce. My heart feels fulfilled when thinking back on the times I could help those who were domestically abused and offered them words of comfort and lead them to a better future by working with the women's association.

My time with a single mother's group was also a growing period for me. There is a primitive limit that is placed on a single parent rearing their children alone. Undoubtedly, there is pain and struggle for children growing up under single parents. There must have been a lot of turmoil in their lives to reach a point of rearing their children alone. That is why single mothers must go through the process of healing themselves and becoming more confident women. At the same time, they need to care for their children by themselves. It is a difficult life, indeed. A single mother's life should not be an individual's problem but a problem that society needs to resolve together. We contemplated how the institution could create a support system for single mothers and increase awareness of the issue. We put our heart into supporting and increasing the individual single mothers' ability to rear their children alone. I also wished that I could be of help to these single mothers in gaining independence and power to support their families.

Single mothers face their own set of discrimination each day. There was a group intended to help women who have divorced their partners or are widowed. It was ordered by Minister K at our church, who was interested in helping those who are in disadvantaged situations and alone. The deaconesses at our church followed this will and organized a group meeting to help them. While the efforts were great, there was covert microaggression towards single women, subtly blaming them for their position. Even within the group itself, there were women that blamed other women for their situations. Widowed women covertly looked down on divorced women and divorced women looked down on single mothers. I am sure no one wants to live unhappily or divorce on purpose. But these women were in the situation they were in either by choice or by circumstance but the main idea we wanted to get across was, that it was not their fault.

The assembly was not intended to belittle these single women by blaming their personalities or actions for the reason for their divorce. Even in a gathering intended to help them, divorced women could not avoid facing judgment and were interrogated to prove that they were not bad people. The gathering was filled with blame and finger-pointing instead of understanding and consolation, and eventually disbanded. After the disbandment, the Korean Women's Association created Dandelion, a group for single mothers and excluded married individuals from joining the group.

In life, there will always be people who rub the wounds of wounded persons and use cruel criteria to hurt and isolate the wounded more from the world. Divorced women face these experiences especially and need to strengthen themselves to stand against them.

I learned how crucial it was to build myself up, gain confidence and strengthen my mental health after seeing some people trying to save their lives with another marriage after failing their first one. It does not matter, I learned, whether you are a man or a woman or married or single; establishing yourself and learning to care for yourself is an important aspect of life. You must not rely on others to save you and build you up; you must look after yourself and become your own saviour. I always emphasized how important it is to go through self-development. One needs to grow the strength to face the world alone, and only then can one fight prejudice and unfair treatment, and that was why I encouraged their independent development.

Thankfully, my children grew up well. They were relatively successful and lived a comfortable life. My oldest daughter worked in England as an international marketing manager, and my oldest son also worked in England as an actuary and a financial advisor. My youngest son was a TV commercial composer and created movies and operas for the stage. When the Korean community found this out, they reacted as if something unbelievable had happened.

"How did your children grow up so successful when you parented them alone, as a single mother?" They would ask.

The words were filled with envy at first, but underneath it, people found it hard to believe that a divorced single mother could parent children so well on her own. Instead of acknowledging single parents for parenting their children successfully despite the tough circumstances, people questioned how it was possible with disbelief. I did not wish other single mothers to experience what I went through, and I told them repeatedly so they could learn from my mistakes.

They must hold on to their dignity and keep their head held high to balance themselves in this world. That was the knowledge I gave to them because I believed this to be true with my whole heart.

When life sways due to heavy responsibility, one looks for something to rely on, a saviour. It's a normal human reaction, I believe. But when you develop yourself to stand tall, you become surer of yourself and your method to face the world. You no longer try hard to be loved by others, and you learn how to share the overflowing love within you with those around you. I cried and laughed with single mothers, hoping that they could face the world with confidence. I grew alongside their growth. As I watched them grow, I sometimes felt the same feeling I felt when my students would grow to be better individuals and set foot towards a brighter future.

Since I never stopped reading or writing, I participated actively in the Korean Writers Association of Canada (KWAC). I structured the organization of the association while running as the president of the association. Through restructuring, we created a separate department for poems and essay subjects and had monthly meetings. Every quarter, we released newsletters to share updates about the association's members and released new works of literature. I encouraged more people to write since I knew that everyone had stories they could share with others.

There is a saying in my language that everyone becomes a poet and a writer as they live. It must be a testament that living is a series of different stories and experiences. Even if no one reads your story, through writing, one can reflect on their life and tend to their pains from the past. You learn more about yourself by reading the words you wrote, and you can reflect on yourself more objectively as well. Through consistent conversation with yourself, you can also grow the strength to protect yourself, so I initiated small writing classes to open the path for more people to write about their stories.

With about 120 participants from the KWAC, we opened a workshop exploring the theme of acceptance and revitalization of overseas Korean Literature. The Korean consulate and the Korean Daily Mail in Toronto sponsored the workshop actively, which allowed writers in Korea and Yanbian, China to participate in the workshop as well. It was an event that allowed Korean literary culture to be known broadly across North America. It was an effort to improve the relationship with the different cultures we interacted with in this land and overcome the limitations that inevitably existed from cultural differences. Through the power of literature, we learned about the ways of others and considered ways to live together in harmony. On a small scale, it improved the understanding of the Korean Canadian community, and on a bigger scale, it was a time for us to recover our love and affection for all human beings.

I was finally faced with my old self, whom I missed dearly. 'Yes, this is who I was originally. I was a passionate person who loved to mingle with others.' We are ironically hurt by people around us and feel solitude among people, but we must never stop living and interacting with others. We must never stop trying to understand one another because we cannot communicate in the same language. We must not forget how to love, and we must not forget that we deserve love. That is just my humble opinion, but it is a philosophy I live by to this day.

I was distant from people for a long time out of fear. Thankfully, I realized that to see darkness clearly, you must get used to the darkness. Only then can you see in the dark. Once you can see clearly in the darkness, you can find your path without getting lost. I tried to find the path I must follow in my own darkness and found my way. Now, I am trying to use the power of self-love to love others. If I can muster up the courage to approach others, and trust others again, then I can seep in with love and finally find myself in that process.

Here, Again, With a Blooming Heart...

Writing was the only form of luxury I could have. Writing was the only thing that helped me breathe when I felt suffocated by my surroundings. That was why I could not stop ruminating and writing even when waves of work overcame me, and I could barely keep my eyes open. I was exposed to a new world by working at the Korean Canadian Women's Association and KWCA. I witnessed how different people in different stages of life lived, and what they thought. It was a precious time.

The 1990s were filled with endless joy, enlightenment, and amazement. My vast forest of thoughts expanded through meeting and learning with experts from various fields. I felt my thirst for learning wake up from deep inside of me as I conversed with more people and organized my thoughts by writing and reading other people's musings. The seed was planted in my heart long before I realized it and it was beginning to sprout. They say no matter where you are, you will always meet your destined one. The seed sowed deep in my heart was asleep all this time, not dead, and it was finally time for it to wake up and sprout its leaves.

The dream of 'learning and exploring a new world' I had when I first set foot on this land was finally reawakening. At first, it was difficult to focus on my English studies, which I started as per my daughter's request, but once I put my heart to it, I could feel my enthusiasm towards learning soar.

I was already forty-nine by this time, but this did not bother me at all. I was excited thinking about what to study, what to be, and what I would be good at as if I was a student about to start freshmen year in university or a new grad about to start my first career. I contemplated hard, looking for the best options and researched actively.

Most people responded negatively to my enthusiasm.

"If you start studying now, when will you graduate?" they asked.

"Can you even finish your studies?" they wondered.

"You should just focus on volunteering for now, forget studying." they suggested.

They judged my decision with dazzling negativity. Their words predicted the impossibility of my dream, but I was confident about my decision and future. My heart was about to explode with anticipation for the education I was about to begin. Other people's concern that my age was too advanced for me to start studying again did not surpass my desire to face the next twenty to thirty years as a better individual. I was afraid as well. There was the burden of learning in a different language, English, and I also had been away from the world of academia for some time. The world had also changed greatly since I studied last, so it was difficult to determine what society expected from this new generation. Nevertheless, all this worry about what and how to start, how to overcome these burdens, and the time spent trying to resolve these worries all made my heart flutter.

Of many subjects to study, psychology and theology caught my interest, but the burden of studying these subjects in English floored me. I decided to use my biology degree at TCM (Traditional Chinese Medicine) University after looking at different program options. I also had this thought that without expertise in certain industries, it would be arduous to survive in this world. I needed a professional career in any field, even just to satisfy myself. I picked science, thinking that the subject would require less language use compared to a humanities discipline, and it minimized the burden I had about learning in English. I encouraged myself, thinking that since I had already majored in biology, I already knew basic jargon in the field and had a belief that I would do fine at TCM. And so, I began my studies.

I spent hours sitting, reading a book, without realizing that my bottoms were bruised. I only realized when taking a shower one day, a blue bruise on one side of my behind. I reflected on the past few days, trying to remember a time I fell. I realized soon after that the bruise must have formed from countless hours of sitting on the chair. Despite my background in biology, it was not easy to close in on the gaps I had from taking a break from studying for so long. I had no choice but to devote more hours than others since I started later than the other students and also had a language barrier to overcome. Sitting and reading diligently was the only way to overcome my disadvantage.

I did not let go of a book as I sat and looked up the same word repeatedly. Some days, I looked up the same word in the dictionary more than twenty times because I still could not remember what it meant. I felt the limits of my ability deep in my bones, but giving up was not an option. I held the book tighter, trying to overcome these limits with effort. I did not want to let go of the book and could not.

Even though I knew it was not my fault, after the tragedy of my brother and sister-in-law, I lived in guilt. I felt the joy of living for the first time since that event. In the corner of my kitchen, I looked at the textbooks and created my notes in my workbooks with my tiny handwriting. Rereading the pages repeatedly, I felt the joy that only those who dream can achieve. It felt like I was JeongAe from the past, from greener times. I was enjoying myself. All the struggles I faced while studying felt like a luxurious time. I wanted these moments to last forever. I was in my realm. I was flourishing and I did not want it to end.

People around me worried if I could even put my studies to use at my age or worried pre-emptively what a waste of my time it would be if I did not finish my studies. These worries did not hinder the pleasure of learning and my will to achieve something. I reminded myself that I only needed to persevere

DANDELION OF THAT WINTER

when faced with my language barrier, the limits of my physique, and the technology advancements. I lived with the books until I could make the information in the books mine and wield them to my will. It was okay for me to not achieve anything right in that moment. It did not matter whether I had a promised future or not. I could not think that time spent learning was wasted time and that the lessons I put into my head were mine to own. I believed that education was an asset I could pull out of my head any time I wished to summon it. This faith allowed me to study endlessly and make my catalogue of my studies spanning over two sets of notebooks.

It is not a lie when they say your efforts will never betray you, and you cannot win against those who enjoy the game—the countless hours I dedicated soon brought me confidence in my field, filling me with knowledge equivalent to the time I dedicated. Throughout my life, diligence was like a clone to me, a quality I kept close to me over time. Eventually, my diligence and efforts rewarded me with valuable time. Thanks to my endeavours, I was able to earn the trust of my younger colleagues and professors who helped me study. Young students have infinite possibilities, and as infinite as their future may be, they have anxiety about the uncertainty of the future. It is inevitable for them to wander a bit out of uncertainty. Unlike them, I was older, my brain did not work as fast, and I was sore here and there, but I did not have the anxiety and time of wandering that young people are more prone to having. I just sat down and assiduously did what I needed to do. I was thankful. I was proud of myself and appreciated my brain for absorbing as much as I put in.

I am grateful for all my colleagues, director of studies, and professors. They all helped my urge to study without any judgment. There were no unnecessary opinions or negative appraisals, and they simply treated me as a friend who studied hard with the same goal in mind as them. When I came across problems I could not understand, I tackled all night to resolve the problem and attempted not to fall behind. My colleagues would hold their thumbs up and smile at me the next morning to praise my efforts. Even to this day, I am thankful for the care and affection they showed me.

My friends and colleagues did not question why and for what I was studying at my advanced age and just observed me and supported my studies. My time would have been a lot more difficult to endure without them. Instead of giving unwanted bits of advice out of worry, they supported me silently. My fellow students and professors helped only if I asked for help, and they were the driving force behind my ability to complete my studies.

Someone once said that studying is a long, hard battle. Potentially, it is the encouragement of people around us that we receive that helps us win this battle.

How could it be only the efforts of soil and sunlight for the hill to flourish green? It cannot be so green without the efforts of those small leaves breaking through the frozen ground and the sunlight, wind and rain that nourishes the leaves. And it is thanks to the surrounding greeneries the hill can be so green. Just like that, my hill became more verdant and flourished greatly.

Relying On My Self...

After finishing a four-year program at TCM, I left Canada and headed to Beijing, China. I studied abroad alone for one year of clinical studies at the Capital Medical University in Beijing.

The Capital Medicine University was one of the biggest universities in natural science, with fourteen different medical departments and related hospitals. Among them, they had four professional TCM hospitals. TCM hospitals treated people with acupuncture, moxibustion, and Chinese acupressure and prescribed people with Chinese medicine. When you entered the hospital, the air was filled with the smell of decoction. Waking up at 5 a.m. every morning to match the first assessment of the day at 7 a.m. was laborious work, but I began to receive field lessons by treating patients at the hospital. The doctors at the hospital were divided into four tiers based on their experience and treatment period. Since I had just finished my education and started to treat people, I was in the most basic group, but I was still the oldest doctor, even among the novice doctor group.

The Chinese patients valued the experience and treatment period of their doctors. Among the group of doctors I was in, I was often appointed the most by our patients because of my age. The hospital operated in a way that patients lined up in front of the doctor they wanted to be examined by, and based on my wrinkly face, the patients assumed that I had much experience and lined up in front of me. Once they learned I was a novice doctor from Canada, the line in front of me would disperse and gather in front of other doctors. Some of the younger patients who could speak a bit of English would sometimes prefer to be examined by us trainee doctors.

It was often that we would have to let the bad blood out of the body when cupping the patients. I was training with other soon-to-be doctors from Scandinavian countries like Sweden or Norway. Since we were not used to cupping and letting out pooled blood, a scream would escape from time to time when the blood splashed from demonstrating acupuncture work.

In Western medicine, they perform surgery for venous blood in the legs, often found in people who work long hours standing up. In Chinese medicine, they use a thick needle to perform acupuncture to treat it. The regular-sized needles could not be used for the legs as thick legs would push them out, so a bigger-sized needle was necessary for this procedure. It was a highly difficult acupuncture skill. The professors who were experts in acupuncture would lay down a sheet of newspaper on the ground, put a basin on top, and put the patient's leg in the basin to pierce a specific area with the needle. The leg would then let out black and cloudy blood into the basin. Seeing bad blood filling up the basin amused and frightened us trainee doctors. We could not help but let out a sound. The patients were so calm even when being poked with such a big needle, and they did not wince. The doctors performing the procedure would see the way we trainee doctors would wince and scold us for being more fearful than the patients who are undergoing the acupuncture procedure.

In Chinese medicine, practitioners focus on blood flow and often use cupping and acupuncture. Even when treating pimples on the face, they may poke the cardinal point at the top of the ear to remove bad blood. It is amazing and fascinating how analyzing the blood flow and puncturing the impacted area directly or treating the acupoint, which can be the source of illness, can help treat a person. I was also amazed at the cupping method, which can let out all the bad blood pooled in the body without surgery. I practiced every day in awe, gradually developing my

DANDELION OF THAT WINTER

skills and expertise as I treated countless patients from seven in the morning to five in the afternoon.

I spent a considerable amount of time training to become a skilled doctor. During my training, I had the opportunity to oversee an acupuncture procedure on the stomach, just below the belly button, which is considered to be a relatively safe area. With my hand full of needles, I focused on the acupoint of the patient while my supervising professor watched over me. As I worked, I admired my professor's skill as he performed numerous procedures in the more risk-prone upper side of the stomach. I was determined to reach his level of expertise one day.

In Canada, acupuncturists use sanitized, one-time-use needles for the procedure. However, in China, clinics usually reuse needles after sanitizing them. A separate health professional is responsible for sanitizing the needles, which are categorized according to their size and disinfected using boiling water. While we do have one-time-use needles available in China, they are expensive and typically used by wealthier patients or foreigners unaccustomed to reusing needles after disinfecting.

In China, my hard work and patience paid off when a French patient visited me, and I finally realized the fruits of my labor. While working as a research assistant at Beijing University, she suffered from insomnia and indigestion and visited the hospital seeking relief. The experienced Chinese doctors treated her with acupuncture, placing a needle on her head to relieve her headache. However, when she returned to the hospital three to four days later, she expressed that there was no improvement. It was during this time that I met her, waiting outside the office after receiving the same treatment as her.

During times when our business was overwhelmed with customers, finding the time to take a break or even have a glass of water was difficult. As a result, we did not always have the opportunity to sit patiently in the office and consult issues in-depth. Each treatment room had around four beds, and patients would lay there waiting patiently for the doctor to come by. In

Toronto, clinics tend to take more time for history taking. However, the doctors at TCM typically asked a couple of questions and performed the necessary procedures on the spot based on their understanding of the patient's condition. Due to this difference in approach, the French patient was not given adequate time to express her symptoms and provide a detailed medical history.

Approaching the patient, I asked her several questions to determine the underlying causes of her indigestion, insomnia, and headaches. After careful examination, I discovered that her eating habits were the main issue. Being unaccustomed to the traditional Chinese spice, Five Spice, I believed this had caused her problems. However, this was not the only issue at hand. The French patient was also experiencing stress due to her unfamiliarity with foreign cultures and languages.

I presented the patient's history to my supervisor and suggested that her stomach and liver may be affected by the stress and food and should be treated accordingly. My words were heard, and my professor assigned me to oversee her treatment. After several days of treatment, the patient's symptoms improved greatly, and my professor respectfully referred to me as Doctor Park.

It was a proud and rewarding moment for me because I was able to relieve a patient from their illness and pain. I felt a great sense of accomplishment because it seemed like my professor acknowledged me as a fellow doctor. I was overjoyed to say the least. After overcoming the physical limits of studying in old age, my experience from life and wisdom from maturity resurfaced to aid me greatly. I researched every day not to trap myself in the teachings of textbooks but to use the information I acquired in practice effectively and creatively.

The acquired life lessons guided my creativity and helped me apply my knowledge to real life. They say that all moments of your life have their own meaning, and it felt like I was being rewarded for all the time I lived in the past.

DANDELION OF THAT WINTER

Studying abroad in China after the age of fifty was a challenging experience. I spent many days hungry in China, a heaven of cuisine, because I was not accustomed to mainland China's traditional ingredients and cooking methods. Until then, I had only tasted Westernized or localized Chinese food.

Local Chinese doctors invited me over for dinner from time to time, but it was not easy for me to eat their food because of the uniqueness of traditional Chinese cuisine. I wondered if this is how the local Canadians felt when I invited them over for Korean food. My colleagues were worried since I was alone and packed food for me from time to time. I could not refuse their care and brought it home and shared it with other Korean international students who lived in the same building as me.

I was busy studying and working in clinics, but on the rare times I had free time, I would go to McDonalds or satisfy myself by visiting the Japanese restaurants in town, although it was quite pricey. I got by each day by eating roasted sweet potatoes, chestnuts, and fruits, all of which had no spices added, and consoled my homesickness occasionally at Korean restaurants.

Slowly but surely, I was filling this precious time I had with knowledge. Once, an older cousin of mine visited me in Beijing from Los Angeles. I stayed in a five-star hotel with her for a week and temporarily enjoyed Chinese food to my heart's content. The hotel had many foreign guests staying, and they altered the spices used in dishes to fit the taste of their foreign customers. All the dishes suited my taste, and I could eat a satisfying amount on top of having the joy of catching up with my older cousin for the first time in a long time.

The knowledge in my head was an asset I could utilize whenever needed. The joy of seeing the quantity and quality of my knowledge improve over time could not be compared to the satisfaction of seeing my material assets grow; it was much more precious. This was the reason I could endure the hard training in yet another foreign land. I feel that I am most alive when I am learning and training in something; it brings me joy. That is why

I cannot stop myself from learning and challenging myself even to this day.

It was spring for me again. I lived on without thinking about my age. Time could age my body, but if I did not reside in my comfort zone and consistently explore and challenge myself, it would be forever spring. I was in my prime as long as I never stopped studying – which would help me bloom into the scintillating flower that was well-deserved.

It was time for me to flower, to reach my full potential and continue to learn and grow. I had come full circle. It took me many years to get here but that does not matter. I am here now and ready to challenge myself and take on whatever comes my way.

PART 4

My Story Approaches its Closing

Not A Recollection, But A Memory...

No tree on Earth has never been swayed by the wind or suffered through a snowstorm. And there are no trees with branches so high and roots so deep in the soil that they bear no scars. Trees endure these painful times, growing taller and becoming an enormous comfort spot for other beings. People are the same. Through experiences and suffering, they inevitably become stronger. It would be beneficial if we could only experience positive situations and learn and grow from them, but it would be hard to complete our lives without experiencing pain. Because some of us have overcome these painful times triumphantly, our past can be remembered as proud and precious moments, and our painful past can no longer hurt us. I see my life's circumstances as a learning curve. It helped me grow big and tall just like the tree standing majestically in the forest.

Looking back, I realize that all the moments of happiness, sorrow, agony, anger, and joy I have experienced have become a memory. It surprises me to see how real and vivid these past feelings are when I dig out the deeply buried memories in my heart. I had intentionally pushed down the painful and numbing emotions and tried to focus only on the good moments. I lived as if I did not remember or recognize my past self and tried to live in the present by cherishing the calm and pleasant moments.

But as I watched my children grow up, I wondered if these memories were mine alone or if they were shared by others who were there with me in the past. I thought that people who have experienced those chaotic waves with me may still be suffering in the memory of the past. And this thought came as a reality when I went to Spain with my daughter.

It was time for me to face my past self. I was being a pushover to unfortunate circumstances and a doormat to some people because I was too foolish to take care of my own life properly. That is why I needed to face my past self and resolve things no matter how much I did not wish to. I needed to muster up the courage for my children, who have protected our family during those tumultuous times. As my husband and I lived together in ridiculous conditions, perhaps my husband and our children had to pay their dues in their way as much as I have suffered. I knew we could be free from these depressing memories once I could face this time straight on, so I gathered the courage. All broken things sound when they break, but my husband and I did not notice the sound of our hearts breaking. We remained silent to the sound of our hearts ripping apart. Our children tried to endure and withstand the turmoil without making any sound between my husband's and my ignorance. It was time for me to help sweeten the sour taste upon my children's tongues after they had suffered for so long.

Poet No Hae Park once said, "To share the love we suffer together, to share the happiness we endure sorrows together, and to share the hope we go through despair together." These words resonate with me deeply, and I have shared my story with my loved ones and those around me in the hopes of finding comfort and connection. At first, I was too afraid to confront my past. I worried that reliving painful memories would only cause more heartache and that others would judge me for bringing up old wounds. But the desire to heal and reconcile was stronger than my fear. With the encouragement of my children, I began to face my past and open myself up to the possibility of forgiveness and understanding.

To most people, one's family is a group of individuals that you need to care for with all your love all your life. My husband and my relationship ended once we were divorced, so we are no longer part of each other's family in legal terms. But to our children, he is still their family as their father. My wish for my children to embrace their father with love remained deep in my heart. One of the purposes of writing this story is to ask my children to be lenient towards their father and me, who could not help but act differently from their expectations because of our differences in generation and culture. These are words of consolation, hoping that our children will throw away all our foul memories and only keep the lovable memories close to their hearts. It is the heart of a mother who wishes for forgiveness from her children who did not deserve the burden of life in their formidable years. I am unleashing this story, mostly for them. It is an average story when comparing it to the lives of many around the world but, to me, sharing this story not only helps me seek forgiveness from my children but it also allows me to break free of my fears and hopefully help other women to empower themselves.

There was much fear facing my memories. I was too scared to engage with my memories. I was anxious that the shattered reminders would pierce my heart, and that the darkness locked in my heart would absorb me. I was also worried that bringing up the echoes of the past unwanted memories would seem like I was blaming my husband for all that occurred. I feared that people around me would judge me and say that I was pretending to be noble now that my life was more at ease. The wish to reconcile was greater than all these worries. I am unsure if it was hatred, regret, blame, or guilt, but I wanted to unleash all these burdens and open myself up. It was thanks to the encouragement of my children that I was able to start facing my past. I could not reject my children's wish to understand their parents and be in touch with their Korean roots, which was difficult because of differences in culture, language, and generation. This project was no longer just a personal work to heal myself. Still, I had another call to close the cultural, emotional and language gaps between our children's generation and our generation. As well, my desire was to empower women by validating their self-expression as I am doing by telling my story. Women's narratives are vastly underrepresented. I hope to spark other women to tell their stories either through written narratives or acting in other ways by getting involved in organizations that are meaningful to them. For me it was the Korean Women's Association but to others it may be getting involved with women's poverty groups, support groups for domestic violence and sexual assault, groups that fight for gender inequality and other wonderful organizations striving to make changes for the betterment of women and their quality of life.

This story is not just my own story. I think that someone out there may have experienced similar experiences as me. There is someone out there who shares my same loneliness, unsaid and hard-to-endure loneliness. This story is intended to comfort those who are miserable and lonely after creating a family, and it is to share with them, console them and encourage them. I am sure that no husband is happy while his wife is unhappy, and no wife is content while her husband is miserable. They just may not know how to express their feelings and share words of consolation. I presume there are more cases where couples are unhappy because they do not know how to communicate their feelings. I also think that when people hurt one another, it is not necessarily because they wish to harm the other person; it may be their struggle to overcome their hurt, and it may have been an immature method of asking for attention.

My husband was invariably unhappy throughout his time with his family. What did he wish to say? But most importantly, why could he not say what he felt? Was it me? Did I not allow him to be able to communicate honestly? Or was it a systemic problem that all males face? I can only surmise that we lived through a turbulent era. Every generation has its generational burden and weight, but our youth was particularly cold, hungry and bleak. That is the time my husband also lived through. I question how much I tried to understand his adolescence filled with bloody violence and fear, his youth crushed with the weight and burden of responsibility, his adulthood, forced to neglect his tenderness and having to be strong, his mid-life, lonely from stubbornness and self-righteousness, and his old age, unable to understand others and be understood, stranded from others. I questioned myself numerous times. How much of my weight and emotion did I attempt to tell him? I tried my hardest to just endure everything instead of letting him know what I was going through and making him understand. I protected myself with pride and used my will to endure everything because I did not wish to show him my weakness. Perhaps that negated his chance to comfort me and help me. Many what ifs tail one another when I think about past moments with my husband.

I was not willing back then to tackle and overcome his wrongdoings. Nor was I willing to tackle my fears. They say neglect is scarier than hate, and I let him do whatever he wished to do with little care because of my own insecurities. It was difficult enough to parent our children, so I avoided fights with him every chance I had. But when I spoke my mind, I needed to fight with him like a crazy person and communicate our problems in inappropriate manners because I felt this was the only way to get my message across to him. Two different people cannot live together without proper communication. Our conversations could not always be pleasant, but I avoided conversing with him, blaming his violent methods. I am part of the blame for why we disconnected.

In some respects, my husband was as headstrong as me. When he started his business, he never slacked on his tax reports. He was always thorough and accurate with numbers, reported his earnings honestly, and paid his taxes accordingly. About five years after he started his business, there was a surprise audit from the provincial government. While most Korean business owners were fined for their inaccurate tax reports, my husband's honesty resulted in a tax return. His accounting abilities were immaculate, and the auditors who did the inspection were disappointed that he did not use his aptness for accounting in his daily life as part of a lucrative career. Their words reminded me of a different side of him, who was always expected to do great things by his colleagues due to his outstanding academic achievements.

My husband must have longed to study deep in his heart for a long time because he had to give up what he was best at out of the burden of supporting his family as the house's patriarch. My heart feels heavy when I reflect on this. I sometimes think that if I tried to acknowledge his sacrifices, perhaps our life would have turned out differently. I will never know if his life was also dictated by the pressure of his generation and had to give up his way of living despite my thinking that he lived freely. He did not know how to spend money frivolously and had no interest in clothes or other material things, but he particularly disliked it when people called him by his name for some reason. He may have had another name he dreamed the world would call him by. Back then, I thought he was being picky for no reason, but I did not think to ask him why. He was a prideful man, and I must have been hurting his pride all along by neglecting him because I did not want to fight so I avoided important discussions that might have helped our relationship. I will never really know, and I know there is no point in wondering and going over "what ifs" but these critiques of my past help me be a better person today. Self improvement is always on my mind so I do not mind going over where I may have gone wrong. The way I see it, it is a learning curve.

Once, he randomly called me, "Honey!" Ridiculously enough, my response to him was, "Have you gone mad?" The words blurted out of my mouth when I heard him call me by an endearing name I had never heard of. His face turned white, then red out of embarrassment, and he turned around angrily. It was not that I disliked him calling me that, but I was flustered. It is a moment in our past that I feel sorry for him and regret even after all this time. I also think if I had let my guard down around him, been softer and welcoming to him, he would have changed as well. I wonder how different things could have been If I did not act like his teacher there to discipline him or his mother, always preparing his meals and looking after him. Would things have been different if I had acted as a woman equal to him and his life partner instead of his mother and teacher? Of course, I can not take the entire blame for our demise. It takes two to tango, as they say. It was as much his responsibility to work on our relationship as it was mine. The dictionary defines marriage as a legal union of two people as partners in a personal relationship. The key word there is partners. Equal partners. The responsibility falls on the two parties involved, and I am very much aware of that fact.

His second wife was different from me. She faced his violence actively, head on. She fought with all her might to stand up against her husband, who was doing unacceptable things to her as a husband. And she left him without hesitation. Not all her actions could be justified, but her assertive method changed her husband in some respects. I sent my children to their place from time to time when they wanted the children to visit since their children and mine are stepsiblings. One time, my children returned from their place and told me that the windows in the house were shattered and that my ex-husband had to call the police. He had been abusing his young second wife the same way he did to me. His younger wife then held up a rock and began smashing all the windows in the house and faced my ex-husband's violence with violence. She grabbed him by the hair and swung him around as resistance against his abuse. My ex-husband eventually had to call the police because she was out of control, and he could not calm her down. When I heard that, I was amazed by her. In some areas, I even looked up to her.

She once said to him, "I have slaughtered all edible animals in China and only have people left to kill. If you hit me one more time, I will take that as a chance to kill you." Her words made me envy her bravery.

More than anything, I was surprised to hear that my ex-husband stopped his abuse after her retaliation. Her behaviour contrasted my old self, who just tolerated everything by neglect because I did not wish to stoop to his level. It is not that I tolerated his abuse for his sake or because I understood him. I did not wish to stoop to his level and avoided the situation by saying to myself, "You avoid things not because you are scared but because it is dirty."

After his younger wife left, the people around us uniformly suggested we get back together. I refused my husband's suggestion to reunite, explaining that I did not wish to be a spare tire. I think he did not expect I would refuse. We were in his car at the time and his hands began to shake while driving, and the car waivered momentarily. He was accustomed to me waiting around even after his countless affairs and did not dare imagine that I would refuse his offer. He made an excuse that he was now reborn as a brand-new person and expressed his discomfort when I said that I believed nothing had changed about him.

My daughter waited for me at home with all the lights turned on when I returned from the conversation with my husband in his car about reuniting. She rushed me into the house. As soon as I set foot in the house, she asked if I would live with her father again with a stern face. Although I said no, she must not have trusted me because she insisted it was my choice to reunite with her father, so she would not interfere, but stressed that she would never set foot in the house if we were to reunite. She expressed her objection strongly, explaining that although she would not come to our home, I could always visit her place. I could not ignore her feelings, but my heart also did not waiver at the thought of reconciling with my ex-husband. I had already cut my ties with him and focused my efforts on healing myself, and I did not wish to go back into the maelstrom with my husband. I knew I would be sucked down a dark well if I were to go back to him. Even though I had gone through some personal development, and I was a different person by this point, that part of my life was over. I needed to move on.

I wondered if there was such a thing as a beautiful divorce. It was a shame that after our divorce, we could not wish each other happiness and cherish the good memories we shared. Maybe those beautiful partings only exist in movies. When I look at Western couples, some still stay as friends after breaking up, but I have no clue if it only seems like that on the outside or if they have a different side to the story when I dig deeper. No matter how painful the breakup was, I did not wish to hurt each other with harsh words and pray for his misery. He and I divorced suddenly, like an unexpected storm, because we needed to, he needed to, so we never had any closure. That may have been our chance to part ways and have closure, but once again, we turned away from each other with no words. We both did not know where to start or how to end things and failed to unload our baggage and showed our clifflike backs to one another. I can not reiterate the importance of communication instead of avoidance.

After all this time, perhaps I was giving my husband the cold shoulder with my neglect to maintain my dignity. He was a smart man, so it was hard for him not to notice my intent. He must have been hurt by my neglect and rejection. He must have felt despair looking at the wall I built between him and me and seeing that I would not budge no matter what he did. It is not only that I could not change because he did not change, but he also could not change who he was because I did not. I do not know if I was tolerating him or evading him. Some say that neglect is crueler than disliking a person. I sometimes feel sorrowful and remorseful that my indifference may have caused him to explode and take away his chance to return to being a good man.

His second wife used the opportunity while my husband was in the United States for a couple of days, attending a conference, to leave with everything they had amassed and filed for divorce immediately. I do not know if she had any ulterior motives, to begin with, but she ended things with him boldly with no regret after realizing that their marriage was not what she had expected. It may be a common thing to do for today's generation of people, but in our generation, once you married, you had to live with your partner, rain or sunshine, so her puzzling departure was devastating to him. I guess she did not have much regret or expectation from that marriage since she did not invest as much time or effort as I did. Her method and decision to leave confused me at how different we were. I wonder if the void he felt when he returned to the empty house was like the futility I felt about the genuineness of our love. I looked back on my time with my husband. We dragged on for such a long time despite having no passion for one another, unable to cut each other out although our feelings were empty.

Once he divorced his second wife, he began to visit me often, uninvited by me and yet pretending to be my husband. I speculate that he thought I would take him back in a heartbeat once he was divorced and did not take my refusal seriously. He came by my work and home and would flaunt his anger that soon enough, our children began to worry for my safety. My daughter felt uneasy by my husband's constant visits and reached out to a lawyer to send my husband a restraining order. I was dismayed by this unimaginable but necessary method, and he was furious. My daughter's action made my husband realize that even his children have turned against him and thus he gave up his reuniting efforts.

Soon after my husband relinquished his reuniting endeavours, his friend introduced him to a different woman, and he married her soon after. I heard that they were of the same age, she was a devout Christian, and they had a big fancy wedding in New York. For his new wife, this was her first marriage, and she changed him greatly. She did not hesitate to call the police when he showed his violent side. He stopped treating her poorly and soon transformed into a docile husband and sincere Christian. It must have been difficult to end his old habits, but I assume it was possible because they were sincere about living together as a married couple and getting accustomed to one another. Instead of expecting that things will get better without doing anything, they must have faced their problems directly to get through their marriage eagerly.

It is all in the past now, and I sometimes think about what use all these thoughts are, but when I try to look at the past from his perspective, I can feel my sorrows and resentment fade away. We married because my husband said he would die if he did not marry me, and later, he betrayed our love, but once I observed him as an individual, I could objectively see his immaturity and weakness. I could even see the fear and loneliness hidden behind his tough exterior. I could see myself in him, knowing I was as immature and weak as he was. I could read how unwise our time together was, and I began to pity his life as much as I had pitied mine.

Just how many couples like him and I existed in our generation? Now, there are a lot of organizations to help married couples who are inexperienced and lack communication skills. Nevertheless, there are still lots of couples out there who suffer from the discomfort of their relationship. I want my story to be a small trigger for them to look after themselves and the people around them. If they face hardships they cannot overcome alone, I ask that they put away their pride momentarily and knock around for someone to help them. After many years have passed, I am reminiscing numerous what-ifs, and I hope that people who are going through hard times right now can try out one of my what-ifs for the people around them. It may make a difference.

My memory ties together my painful life. These memories now remain in me as vistas of my life. People do not get older. They merely age. They say that one really becomes old when their heart gets older. What does it mean for your heart to get older? I think we truly get old when we lose the bravery to face the world we are in, or when we let go of the adventurer in us because of our comfortability, and when we forget the feeling of our hearts fluttering by meeting new people and the world with love. We must not stop laughing, talking, fighting, and reconciling with the people around us. We are no longer alive when we stop our interaction with the world. We need to open ourselves up to accept the world and the people. We do not need to be disappointed or complain that the world or other people are not coming to us even when we reveal ourselves. All we need to do is step forward towards the world and the people around us.

Strong Yearning...

Longing is a memory. Just like how we have faces we miss and people we long for, I have times that I miss. Many out there reminisce about their past, thinking, 'It was great back then.' What are we longing for in the past? We may miss the people we spent time with together, but perhaps we miss ourselves in more than anything. I must have been happy during that time. I must have loved the people I was with and brought joy to them, most definitely. It is unclear if I wish to return to my old self or miss the times back then, but it brings a smile to my eyes when I think back on those fond moments, no matter how much time has passed.

I miss the time when I was pregnant with my first child the most. Every moment felt like sunshine with pure happiness. I embraced the baby in me by only thinking about good things, saying nice words, and being cautious of what I ate, and how I acted. I can still feel the happiness of that time vividly and I miss it dearly. My life was fulfilled from loving my baby. It was a time I loved everyone with a thankful heart. Once I avoided negative thoughts for the baby in me, all my actions naturally came from a place of love toward others. I thought that once this baby was born, I would finally be complete, and I would never die. My two sons may be disappointed to hear this, but the overwhelming gratitude my first child gave me was unlike any other. The excitement I felt when knitting my baby's clothes and the butterflies from her movement in my stomach brought me complete happiness. Even today, that feeling is so vivid and brings me calm and longing.

School is an environment I am used to, and I am fond of. My first job was teaching at a school. Since I spent several years studying and returned to school to teach, I have a lot more memories at school compared to others. The people I met in school visit my thoughts from time to time, but my time during high school is more clear and vivid than any other memory. I miss my friends with whom I spent those gem-like times together. I have met many people in my life under the name of friends or acquaintances and have since parted ways with them. My friends from high school particularly stuck around in my memory more than others.

Both my friends and I were pure and innocent. We had nothing but our hearts and only had our hearts to give. We shared everything with each other. I would even share of pod of peas with them if it came to that. But we only had our hearts of offer as those times were difficult, but we would do so willingly.

Although we have more freedom now with more time and materials to share, we have become increasingly stingier about sharing our hearts. Even while sharing our belongings and time, it has become more difficult to share our feelings. That is probably why I missed the time when we shared everything with one another. They say feelings are something we can share anytime since we all have them, but I think it is one of the most difficult things to share. It is true that as we become greedier and more calculative, our pure hearts have smaller occupancy within us. We hide our caring hearts because we do not want to lose out on the relationship, and sometimes, it becomes difficult to find because of how well hidden our caring hearts are. Sometimes, we even forget that we hid them and believe we never had these caring hearts to begin with.

My memory with my high school friends is more precious because we did not need to hide our feelings from each other and shared only innocence with each other. It was a time when

DANDELION OF THAT WINTER

we were unafraid to try new things, and we did not despair over failures. Instead of picking at each other's faults, we comforted each other. That is why our hearts were always rich despite not having much. We had nothing but our hearts which did not diminish no matter how much we shared and gave away. I missed those pure hearts, and that longing eventually led me to KCPCAC (Korean Canadian Physically Challenged Adults Community). It was a relationship that could only be fully formed once we shared our hearts.

I made ties with the organization in 1997 when it was founded, and I am with them today. Just like the book titled *Accompany*, released in celebration of their twenty-third anniversary, I accompanied them all this time, and it is the organization I will accompany for the rest of my life. I feel indebted to them occasionally because I do not feel I have accomplished much during my two terms as the chairmen of the organization. I dream of a world where disabled adults are not hurt by society's opinions and ignorance. I hope they can mingle with people and live on while laughing and crying. I wish that I could accompany them towards a better world. I worked with many different organizations in the immigrant community. However, KCPCAC feels particularly close to home because of how much help it still requires, unlike other organizations that have settled comfortably thanks to many great individuals who led the organizations.

I am also thankful that my students at TCM University have all graduated and are settling well in their fields. Some of the graduate students have consistently volunteered to treat those in need. It is possible to volunteer once or twice because of other people's recommendations, but it is difficult to spend five, ten or even fifteen years without devoting your heart to it. Because I know how difficult it is to pledge yourself to volunteering for such a long time, I am proud of all my former students.

When refugee families from North Korea arrived in Toronto in 2010, we were fortunate enough to have access to our former student clinics that operated for free once a week. We immediately began offering treatment services to North Korean refugees and the disabled. Our commitment to the cause was so strong that even when the weather was too cold or the patients had difficulty walking, the doctors would visit their homes personally to offer treatment. On occasion, when we were overwhelmed with patients, my apartment would become a makeshift clinic. The most common complaints we received from North Korean refugees were related to arthritis and pneumonia, while disabled adults typically suffered from infantile paralysis. We also treated a significant number of patients who had suffered from strokes or accidents that left them disabled. Being able to offer our services to those who needed them brought me immense joy and happiness, and it added depth to my life. They are also the reason I was passionate about learning Chinese medicine. The meaning of my life has become much clearer through volunteering. It is something I should be thankful for instead of being thanked for my services.

We could not hide our disappointment when we had to shut down our free clinic, which had been operating for fifteen years, because of unforeseen circumstances. The pandemic forced my former students' clinics to shut down, and I felt devastated that we could not even visit our patients' homes. We could not help those who needed medical care because we could not secure the space to offer medical attention, so securing a space for the sick became the main request of my prayers. Although we will be slowed down by a momentary set-back, it will not be a difficult path, and our time now will shine brightly in the future as a distant memory.

People these days often use the word 'male friend' or 'female friend.' Life has significantly changed. My generation welcomed modernization, but we were still tied down by gender stereotypes and the belief that men are superior to women. I find this new slang refreshing and cool. There was a time I met a friend who shared my last name. We hung out like cousins with no burden and had a "thing." He was a friend whom I met when I was still

DANDELION OF THAT WINTER

inexperienced, and he made me feel butterflies from time to time. Unfortunately, during my time with him, friendship between men and women was not allowed, let alone any in-between feelings of love and friendship. I had to end things without really starting anything, but I miss how pure and innocent I was back then. I miss the days when I believed in people's feelings and trusted the heartful exchange between men and women. These memories are like fall leaves that colour my heart and bring sweet winds from time to time.

My marriage with my husband was when I could not help but deny that love existed. It was a time I confirmed every moment of how weak human love can be. I was rigid and inflexible emotionally, and it was burdensome to witness my husband's everchanging emotions and enormous maelstrom of feelings. Once settled, my feelings did not sway and stayed in the same space, but in my husband's emotional chaos and ocean of feelings, I would often be lost. My husband did not realize the layers and extent of feelings, and of course, he did not know how to organize and express all those feelings. Since we did not try to learn, we were always stuck in this emotional storm. This time of my life was not pleasant but, if anything, it made me the woman I am today. They say we learn from our struggles, and they can teach you many wonderful lessons. Those struggles built my character and made me stronger. When those struggles were finally over, I was able to remember the person I was, and I could go back to that person I missed so much. But I also transformed into someone new and improved.

During my young adulthood, the situation in my country was dire and unless you were starving or had missing limbs, you were expected to be thankful for what you had, and it was seen as selfish to ask for more. Wanting a relationship with your spouse that involved an exchange of feelings was seen as frivolous and unnecessary. Because of this reason and many other reasons as I have explained, my husband and I were very aloof towards each other and did not share our hearts with one another because we could not understand the need for this exchange. These days, I see young people expanding their experience by meeting various people, dating, and breaking up with them. They meet different people, and through a wider experience pool, they learn the world. I rather envy their ways, and I wish to some degree that it could have been like this for us in those days.

Friendship between the opposite gender was immoral, and friendship for women after marriage was deemed wrong out of fear that women would neglect their household. Since both men and women lacked the experience of forming relationships and learning about people, it could not be helped for marriages to falter quickly over common issues that could easily be rectified with some discourse.

Some will argue that no matter how the world is, there are still numerous people who are living just fine, meaning, they can adapt to any circumstance and make the best of life in any kind of situation. Of course, there are personal differences, and we are all born with different abilities, so there must be some people who can overcome any life changes and some that can not. In that aspect, I am ashamed of my inability and foolishness. It is also why I cannot simply blame my husband's ignorance and incompetence. I am not blaming anyone or making excuses, but it is a shame that we did not have the opportunity to meet a diverse group of people with various educational and cultural backgrounds and gain knowledge from them to help give us strength and wisdom to overcome the difficulties in our relationship. If we had prepared ourselves by gaining worldly experience through the insight of others, we could have overcome the conflicts in our relationship more effectively.

I learned so much worldly knowledge when I was a teacher. It seems ironic to say that I learned the most when I was teaching, but it is true. My mind always goes back in time when I was with my students who taught me well. That time was full of life. It was filled with eyes of eagerness towards learning. With those gazes, I could be truthful to them and truthful towards the world. I miss that time dearly because I know how difficult it is to be purely passionate and what a precious opportunity it is to meet those clear and pure eyes.

I was with students who were as bright as the sky, as passionate as the sun, and as delicate yet resilient as the grass on the hill. I was as bright and warm as the students. We were happy and had a fun time. I did not realize then that I would miss this time dearly many years later. I did not think it would become a cherished memory, bringing a smile to my face when all my efforts felt futile, like many teachers feel, I guess. It is a longing that I am thankful for. I wonder where those children are, whose sky, fence, and sunshine they have become. I do not doubt that wherever they may be, they are someone's beloved individual who cares for others dearly and thank their surroundings.

Even Though I Forget and Moved On...

A myriad of events have taken place. I endured it and overcame it. There was an innumerable amount of pain and hardships, but I lived and overcame my turmoil rather than questioning why this was happening to me and falling into despair. So, I had no regrets, but that may not be the case. There are some regrets even though I have forgotten about most things and lived on.

When I see my children growing up and living happily with their families, I am reminded of how rich my life is, and I am thankful once more. Like any other parent, I gave my best for my children in the given situation. I do not doubt the effort I put towards them. No matter how busy my day was, I prepared home-cooked meals for them and helped them with their homework as much as I could. Even when I could not buy them fancy clothes or accessories, I dressed them in clean, modest clothes to make them presentable. I split my time between baking their snacks and making their home-cooked food with affection.

Despite all this, there is a corner of my heart that feels sorry for my children because we have not been able to make enough adequate memories. We were faced with the wall of reality, stuck in a violent environment, and never had the opportunity to sit together to eat peacefully and exchange conversations, let alone a family trip. There is no recollection of our children being childish towards their parents and playing around the house. It is a shame that we do not have a single happy memory we can say is a shared family memory. As I watch my children all grown up and create memories with their own children, I feel proud and sorry at the same time. It is not something I could have accomplished by myself, but if I had convinced my husband or mustered up some affection to persuade him, we could have planted happy memories of their family in our children. Sometimes, this shame evolved into guilt and made me feel that everything was my fault.

I never once asked my children what their favourite subject was or if they had any hobbies since I was preoccupied with putting food on the table and a roof over their heads and supporting their studies. Some say this is just how it was back then, but a part of my heart still aches when I think about it. Although children attended trips or camps organized by the school or the church, we never dared go on a family trip. We could not even think about closing the store for multiple consecutive days. We were satisfied with visiting a nearby city for one or two days. We did not fully understand what it meant to escape from our daily activities and to spend time with our family. I am embarrassed thinking that we may have just imitated what spending time with family looks like. I am sorry we could not offer them happy memories with their parents for them to look back on and tell their children stories of family vacations.

Regardless of all this guilt, my children grew up to be healthy both mentally and physically and never displayed any disappointment towards me. Sometimes, my face gets hot when looking at their faces, knowing they also knew how their friends' families lived. Fortunately, they never showed signs of envy or rebelliousness.

Memorable memories are made through effort. There are some cases where great memories form naturally, but if your circumstances are not the most favourable, you must take your time creating memories. Looking back later in life, sometimes our efforts become precious memories. As much as we put our heart into it, those souvenir recollections were few and trivial. I hope that people live every moment to create memories to look back on in the future and live the moment.

When looking back on my youth, I regret not meeting numerous people and interacting with them. I had many opportunities to engage with many precious people as I participated more actively in the Korean community. Meeting these few special people I made acquaintances with, made me feel that my life would have been enriched if I had met them earlier.

I am reminded of our elder's words that studying has a time and purpose. Meeting prominent and highly educated people is part of a learning experience because they have wisdom to learn from, so it is necessary to meet peers and enlightened, sophisticated people from your teenage years and up to your eighties and nineties. To consistently learn is why I am busily seeking notable individuals to listen to their thoughts and opinions to improve my insight. Networking and exchanging dialogue with others from various fields of expertise is the best education, in my opinion, next to attending physical classes.

When I was young, the opportunity for women to receive education increased, but society coerced most women to stay at home. The reason for educating women did not lie in women's enlightenment or for them to evolve into valuable members of society, but it lay in transforming them into wise mothers, hence developing decent families. It was difficult for women to enter society after graduating from higher education outside specific industries. The idea that men are superior to women was still emphasized in our society, and many women were still locked up in moral prisons set by the distorted concept of chastity. I was not an exception to this. Unlike most women after wedlock, I had the privilege to work at a school and expand my knowledge and abilities, but I did not dare to escape from the moral prison created by society. I was not ready to challenge this notion. So, I applied a stricter moral compass to myself since my husband was nearby. I locked the doors shut tight in that moral prison. I limited my interaction with male colleagues to an extreme point, so naturally, my interpersonal experiences were limited, and I missed many opportunities to grow as a mature member of society. Not because men are wiser but because I was limiting myself to only half of society.

I do not know if it is a quality I was born with or if it is because I received an education stemming from patriarchal and Confucian culture, but it is still difficult for me to express my deepest feelings. I quietly hid my hurt feelings from everyone since I was taught that not being swayed by the world is a virtue, and that one must not express sadness and happiness openly. My duty was to endure all my hardships silently. I did not doubt these teachings and walled myself from questioning these beliefs because I could abide by the corruption but could not accept that it was wrong. I built a wall high enough to cut myself off from the wall because I judged the world based on the strict moral compass I held. I regret having such a strict dichotomy between right and wrong when looking at the world we live in instead of living more fluidly and flexibly.

For one to be happy in this world, one must explore the differences in the world and build our identity through these experiences to acknowledge the differences in individuals and handle conflicts with flexibility. Humans are lonely beings if they do not connect with other living beings. They need to accept the loneliness rooted deep in themselves and venture forth to meet the world. They say humans are lonely in a crowd, but only when we are with one another can we be popular. We can shine when we have people around us. We must not meet the world as a rebellion against our loneliness. And we must not love someone out of protest to the desolate feelings. If we continue to be lonely and desolate together, eventually, these feelings will become a memory because our togetherness will vanquish our loneliness.

Giving Myself to the Arms of The World...

The world was crude to me one moment, not even giving an inch of generosity, then the next, it embraced me with a vast open heart. When I tried to bind myself to the standards I set up and tried to judge the world based on my principles, the world, without fail, showed its ruthlessness towards me. When I broke down the wall I erected towards the world, the world embraced me with open arms as if it was never ruthless. When I conducted my life with a toxic competitive spirit, the world was brutal, as if it is giving me a lesson to realize my foolishness. If I had let my poor heart flow with the water and passing wind, the world would have become more docile, and it would have become more soothing to live.

Everything depended on me. I should not have let the everchanging world and people decide my happiness. Only after I had parted ways with my husband, I realized my foolishness for being obsessed over a successful and lasting relationship. I needed to accept that the world is not black and white, fix my intolerant perspective, and change my perspective of others to a healthier one. I thought that ending my marriage with my husband meant failure, and I held on to the relationship because I could not accept that I had failed. It may have been because I was an old person believing that we must live with what we were given. I needed to reflect on myself and consider what I did to change him. We parted ways rashly and unintentionally because of the circumstances we were in. It was a new opportunity given to me since I had been too weak and rigid to make any changes, and a moment to end the dead relationship and head towards a new direction.

As I started studying again, I decided how to live from then on. The fulfillment I gained from piling experiences led to self-confidence. My unconscious foolishness to protect my self-esteem based on other people's views disappeared as I did what I could within the organization I was a part of and strengthened myself internally. It was not an easy task. It is not that I do not have moments of weakness, wavering to the opinions of others. There are times when the positive energy in me weakens because of other people's negative opinions about me. No matter how weak I was, I focused on myself and reclaimed my center with serenity and confidence. I hardened slowly on some days and more rapidly on others. It may have taken some time; nevertheless, I always returned to myself. I no longer let others dictate my happiness.

Life is full of contradicting ideas and my life is testimony to that statement. It is inevitable for all hateful relationships to either transform into something better or to end. The maturity to accept that your time with a person has ended allows you to overcome the pain of a breakup and gives you the strength to preserve the primary affection and trust one has for people in general.

I finally had the strength to overcome the ending of my relationship with my husband when I reflected on our relationship from a different perspective, and the negativity towards myself faded away. There was no need to blame anyone or have any unnecessary remorse when I think that we lost the momentum to preserve our relationship healthily and that we have ended the taxing relationship for our happiness. I could let go of the pain and grief that inevitably follow breakups. And in that place, peace and stability found its way once I healed. With a stronger heart, I lost the hesitancy to form new relationships. Every action, experience, trip, hobby, and friend were a new tie for me. Once I became stronger, I had the strength to raise the positive energy I had within me and the warmth I had towards the world and people.

There needs to be warmth in human interaction. Those who cannot love themselves cannot love others. 'If you cannot love others, others cannot love you.' These words sounded like wordplay previously, but now they have settled in my heart. We all need acceptance, respect, and love from those around us. And to achieve this, we must step forward with open arms and embrace the world. If I spread love among people, eventually, that same love will return for me to soak up. Positivity is bidirectional. Spread it to others through positive actions and it will come back to you in a gratuitous cycle of optimism.

I met many pupils while working at TCM for twenty years after graduation. As my interest in acupuncture and Eastern medicine widened, I connected with different doctors, nurses, and physiotherapists as a teacher and pupil. Each one is a precious connection I have made. They are the seeds that will better this world and make it healthier. As the world changes, some medical practices have become commercial tricks, but some more excellent graduates prioritize the value of human life and share the pain with their patients. I know the sincerity they possess because of the time they have invested in volunteering for the sick.

Their outreach efforts have paused because of the global pandemic and lack of space, but I believe they will start again when the circumstances improve. I feel surer of the path that I walk in when I help the sick and share their pain. It is my duty, and it is the path I wish to follow. It is also a path that will be filled with the warmth and kindness of people.

People often say that although their body is old, they are still young at heart. It probably means that aging does not age the soul. It must mean that one only becomes old when one gets too comfortable with one's surroundings and avoids new challenges and adventures. I intend to keep my soul young as I feel the joy of learning and teaching will keep my spirit youthful and my eyes will always shine at new experiences.

I wish to be a free individual, not tied by anything or anyone. I wish to have the strength to be more accommodating about the spikes that have hurt me and be more accepting of the pain brought to me by the world. I wish to root deep down amongst many different people. I want to use the same will and determination I had to protect my children in my past to support and inspire others now. I want to become a big flourishing summer tree for troubled people to rest and heal at and then go on to face the world with resourceful beauty and enthusiasm. Those beautiful faces will shine through the flourishing green leaves and take a fond place in my heart.

PART 5

My Story Concludes for Now

The People Who Made Me Who I Am...

We borrow our parents' bodies to come into this world and encounter and pass-through countless people. Without those interactions, I would not be here today the way I am. That is why every interaction I have experienced transformed me and completed me. Some have brought me anguish, and some brought bliss. Some have lasted a long time, and some only stayed briefly. There are some I do not even wish to remember because of how frustrating our relationship was, but when I think about it, they have also affected me as an individual in some ways. Looking back, each past interaction has fulfilled me through encounters and departures.

Since I do not have much recollection of my father, my mother is someone I do not have enough words to describe. Mother is a precious word for every individual. When I think of the word mother, I am reminded of her sitting politely with her hair in a bun, well brushed with camelia oil. She was educated with modern principles, and it was not because she wore a hanbok with a traditional hairdo that her image of modernity was sacrificed, but her pristine posture and rigid personality often gave me and others that illusion of archaic and antiquated practices.

My mother received higher education during the Japanese colonial era, and she was accustomed to manners and showing respect to others. Because of that, she always presented herself without any faults. She must have been a lot stricter on herself to protect herself and her children because she lost her husband at a young age and had a beautiful appearance. There was no dishevelment in her discipline and education either. I still remember the lessons we had with her once a week. She observed our four siblings keenly throughout the week, wrote down when we were at fault, and picked one day to discipline us. Unlike my sisters, who accepted the punishment without whining, I would run away from the little stick. My mother looked like she could not kill a fly most days, but when she disciplined us, she seemed cold-hearted. I think it came from a place where she felt it necessary to educate us properly, so we did not hear anyone belittling us for not having a father. I am sure a part of her wanted to let us live freely, the way children our age should live, but she needed to ensure we did not hear sneers from people around us for not having a father. I realize now that it was her way to protect us from the harsh words of society and give us strength to live on and I understand this now that I have raised my children.

My mother's moral principles and strong ethics impacted me greatly. It acted as a way for me to decide my principles about how to live my life and accept human nature and duty. How we are taught at home can impact an individual's personality and development. But this was the case especially for me because it gave me the keen eye to decide right and wrong and gave me a strict moral compass to decide that if it is wrong, it is wrong. By learning an honest and patient way of life, I overcame many problems with a willing heart. It became the basis for calmly organizing my emotions and becoming rational. Meanwhile, the challenge of trying new things took precedence before fear or hesitation. In any case, it helped me avoid responding to situations emotionally and wasting my efforts unnecessarily to sabotage the work I had accomplished.

The power of reason I had activated positively whenever I encountered the difficulties of our generation and unfamiliar culture. On the other hand, my reliance on the power of reason made it difficult to express my feelings. I displayed signs of being unable to share my innermost thoughts, and sometimes, I tried to confine people in the moral prison I used to confine myself in. There must be some who found it difficult to match the life standard I had set. As I was not uncomfortable with my strict mother's teachings, I probably treated people with stringent traditions that were no different from my mother's.

I reflected on myself to see if I could accept that everyone's abilities, expectations, and character can be unique, and I tested myself to discover if I had not lost the flexibility of my thought process. To my mother, who hated dirt and distraction in life, my divorce was an act of breaking trust. To this day, I somewhat feel sinful for what I allowed to happen. The reason I maintained my long and difficult marriage was to protect my family, but it was also because I knew how much pain my divorce would bring about to my mother. She told me in the past that she trusted me more than any other children she had. About five years after divorcing my husband, I could not hide it from my mother anymore and told her the truth while lying next to her on a dark and silent night. After hearing my confession, she did not say anything. The weight of silence transformed into a giant boulder and took place in my heart.

Along with my mother, Ahn Changho, known as Dosan by his pen name, also helped me set a certain standard in my life. I learned his ideals at Heungsadan Academy during university, and it helped me create a particular vision for my future and how I will live. He emphasized the need to improve our abilities, and his teachings gave me the strength to never slack on learning. It also became my ideology when teaching children. His honesty that there shall not be a lie even in death pierced my young heart. This became the direction I headed towards as a human being. His words that true penitence comes from changing our minds and behaviour helped me realize the importance of taking action and heightened my challenging spirit throughout my life. His ambitious view stated that we must envision the future of our people in the world, which enriched my desire to explore the bigger world.

Above all, I was very fortunate to have had the opportunity to listen to the lectures of many great visionaries through the activities of the Heungsadan[9] during that time. It was an essential impetus for broadening the scope of learning, which could have been limited at a local university. This is what allowed me to start a challenging study in a foreign language at the age close to fifty and allowed me to focus on my studies in a foreign country at an old age. His will that we must change our behaviour as much as our thoughts to make the world a happier place allowed me to share my abilities with the world and live a life of giving and sharing what I have learned.

It is hard to find the meaning of life without having any purpose. It is challenging to have a happy life with no meaning. It is crucial to meet a good teacher when you have a softness towards the world to set a reason and direction in your life. Your teacher does not need to be great or famous. The world has many hidden experts and treasures yet to be discovered. I wish that everyone could find someone who can make the bell in their head ring and find that teacher to fill their life. As long as we do not stop our thoughts and critical thinking and fear taking on new challenges, we are still young, so it is never too late to try.

There is a person I remember when I talk about sharing. It is Jeongja Shin, whom I call a human angel always. The memory of my childhood takes place in my heart like sunshine, but her life is what I wish to grow to be. It is true that once people succeed socially and become richer materially, it is easy to look down on others and control yourself.

I remember the words of my acquaintance. When they were young, they constantly reprimanded the frivolous spending habits of wealthy people and said that they would spend their money in a classier manner when they became rich. But once they reached

---

[9]   An enlightenment organization founded in 1907, and later reestablished by Ahn Chang-ho in the United States in 1913. It played a significant role in the Korean independence movement. The establishment focused on raising leaders with a commitment to independence, loyalty, and courage.

that level of success, their promise was not fulfilled as they had intended. They smiled awkwardly, explaining that for a long time, they spent their money frivolously, which they detested greatly, and it took a long time to realize that they were doing so. They also said that they were thankful to have realized it before they died, although it took a long time.

Sharing is a difficult task. It is easy to ask others to share what they have, but it is challenging to give up what you have to share with others. On that note, it is a huge privilege to observe Jeongja Shin's life up close. Her life is very privileged. She is the wife of a man who is a chairman at a very well-known hospital in Seoul and has the riches that others would envy but lives modestly. She generously shared what she had with others in need, although she was frugal with her spending. She was always cautious about relying on her societal power to harm others. For sixty years, she sponsored scholarships for needy students and volunteered medically and communally. Others try hard for their children to inherit their success, but she tries to pass down the spirit and practice of sharing with her descendants. Learning how to share is the most beautiful and prized inheritance. I watched her life closely as she emphasized the need to give back to society, especially those who have been educated and have the riches to share. Naturally, I soaked up her ideologies, and although minimal, I tried to follow her steps. Giving and not expecting anything in return gives me great reward.

Sharing is a habit that needs to be developed over many years. It needs dedication and practice. If you make time to share after you become successful, you will need to know when to share, with whom to share and what to share. But most importantly, you must ask yourself, 'why am I sharing?' Are you doing it for the right reasons or to just look good in front of society? I am curious how many people are out there who can explicitly decide that now is the time to share what they have without thinking that sharing is a waste of time and resources. Some people do not know how to share because they lack the practice once they become rich enough to give back. Sometimes, their approach is incorrect, and they may unintentionally hurt other's feelings. Everyone thinks that their very existence is something to share with the world. If you do not have material wealth, you can share your time which is as valuable as that material, and if you do not have enough time to share, you can share your heart and feelings with others that need to speak of their emotions as well. This may be the most difficult to share.

Every day, we see small and big conflicts that are created from not sharing goodness with others. When you see that, there is nothing more expensive than sharing your heart. Some may think that there is no need to share your heart with others because we all have a heart. Some treat the act of sharing hearts as if it is useless, but this is the starting point of everything. If you get into the habit of sharing small things first and sharing your inner most feelings, eventually, everyone will become experts in sharing beautifully and wisely. Try sharing with those around you, to plants and animals, offer them a warm word of care, and see what happens. If you do not know what to say and feel awkward about saying something, even a shy smile is enough. Smile and you shall be smiled upon!

I contemplated how I could share what I have despite having less success or materials as Jeongja. The joy of understanding each other and sharing love brightens my life. My relationship with Jeongja started in middle school. We attended the same high school, and the memories we created together still shine brightly in my mind. Even after all that time, she still inhabits a special place in considerable moments of my life as a beautiful, soft colour and warm rays of light. She gave me the force to live, was a model for me to pursue, and helped me realize the joy of sharing and living with others. I rely on the spiritual awakening and guiding principles I learned from her when I am at my weakest.

My time with various volunteer organizations in the Korean immigration society gave me the life force to live on. All organizations are stemmed from their understanding and

DANDELION OF THAT WINTER

compassion for people and their willingness to help people achieve better lives and give them opportunities that will hopefully lead them on a path to success. Offering the little I have to these organizations is a rewarding time for me. If I can make a positive difference in just one person's life, then that is enough for me. I feel as though my life has purpose and meaning and my life is not wasted.

The one who taught me the pleasure of working for others is Ara Jo from YWCA, whom I met as an adolescent. She has since passed, and I cannot physically see her, but she is always in my heart. She is the secretary general who helped me during challenging moments. She was a born general and, with a bold and passionate personality, offered me countless advice that helped me in favourable ways. Her guidance planted a sense of reality and sound judgment when I was young. She made me cautious of looking at the tree instead of the entire forest and taught me the modesty that if we focus on the now by working hard, our desired future will eventually come. Her bold sense of reality reinforced the positive mindset in me. Because of that, I could use myself in the world with the mindset of 'if I do it, someday I will achieve' without being discouraged. I practiced the momentum to put my thoughts into action by being active at the YWCA with her. It was another learning environment for me to experience by participating in fairs and events that all strive to bring about a better organization. I learned things I could not have understood without experience then. It became my foundation to enact many different organizational activities later in life. In that sense, my relationship with Ara is a blessing and a privilege, giving me the foundation to be where I am today.

It is great luck that I met many great people who improved my life. When I was stuck in darkness and did not know the path to walk, they walked with me like a ray of blessing and gave me the strength to step forward. I am genuinely grateful for them.

In May 1985, Minister Jin Hong Kim visited Toronto for a Christian faith seminar. When he visited, my family and Korean society were still distraught by the tragedy that befell my brother and sister-in-law. It was a dark age for me. The world had turned against me. I felt that even God had forgotten me and barely breathed in the swamp of sadness. I had no relationship with the Minister, but he called me to offer consoling words. It gave me the strength to push out of the swamp I was in. Other than the Minister at the church my in-laws attended, no other minister had offered words of consolation to our family. Everyone pushed me to leave Toronto. Minister Jinhong knew that and said that I must persevere where I am and trust in God. He advised that I remain silent and pray, and only communicate with God and let God take care of everything. He gave me the force of life when I felt that everyone had betrayed me and could not trust the world or God. Minister Kim was a man who breathed the breath of faith into everyone with his soul-stirring living faith. His life did not differ from his words, and he loved those who needed help. I could regenerate with the living faith the Minister breathed into my life. I am even more grateful to Minister Kim Jin-hong because instead of getting rid of the people around me who were making me feel uncomfortable, he gave me the strength to endure on my own.

The extraordinary people who made me who I am today are shining memories in every corner of my life. Even if I cannot remember them all, they are brilliantly engraved in every corner of my heart. That gratitude I keep in my life has inspired me. Because of them, I am able to share my warmth with the world. Through them, the lesson continues to be passed on to others.

My youngest son once said that the world may seem like it is full of bad people, but as long as five percent of the population is made up of kind people, the world continues to spin. My son consoled me by saying that he is happy that we are part of that five percent. I do not know if good and bad people could be categorized strictly in a binary way. And I also do not know if the people who make the world go round are five percent of the population. I was surprised and worried by my son's words that he believes ninety-five percent of people are bad, but it comforted me when he said that life is still okay as long as that five percent continues to shine in the world. "I see, that's all we need," he declared. I was relieved and thankful that such a small light could shine on this great darkness.

There are a lot of harsh and mean people around me, so even though life is hard, and sometimes they make it harder, I can greatly appreciate those few good people who keep me alive and help me move forward with their positivity and goodwill. One small joy can erase a hundred sorrows. I am happy to have those who kept me going through all the hardships and my life moving. Some incredible people enlightened and guided me with a ray of light in the darkness, and I still listen to them. I want to be one of someone's five percent, just like the people who made me. I hope to continue to be one of those five percent in the future. It is important to me that I can make a positive and meaningful difference in someone's life because my desire is to pay it forward, as they say.

The Time It Took to Make Me...

They say time is given relatively to everyone; despite that, time goes by too slowly or fast at times. There are days when I am left dissatisfied with being unable to complete my tasks, although I spend all day long busy and active.

To those who immigrated to a foreign land, every day may have felt brand new, and sometimes, these days may have felt too complex to endure. As difficult as life can be, the desire to take a breather must have been great.

Each person has their way of coping with difficult times. I also have had moments that have helped me tolerate the hardships of life. These times did not only comfort me but helped me grow and move forward.

It was writing. Time spent on writing was also special to me. I loved writing ever since I was a little girl. Perhaps even at a young age, I enjoyed the peacefulness you get after writing your thoughts out. I never had enough time because of our family business and my responsibilities as a wife and mother. I needed to write even when exhausted, and my body asked for rest. That is how I could finally breathe after a long, busy day. My time writing was a time for me to talk with myself, and it was a moment to communicate with the world while being stuck in my suffocating life. It allowed me to breathe when I was lonely and cut off from the rest of the world because of intolerable abuse. I wrote my inner thoughts. I was too embarrassed to voice my thoughts into written words, but I overcame that self-consciousness. With that consolation, I earned the courage to live the next day and strengthened myself.

Writing made me sturdier. It is not that I was writing something grand. I did not write because I knew the healing power and effect that writing had, as people these days say. When I had no one to rely on, the blank piece of paper was the only spring of freedom that I could depend on. It was a field of souls that I could unleash all my heart's content without worrying about what others may think. After pouring out my heart through writing, I reflected on myself by reading what I had written. It gave me an objective insight into the situation I was in. These times had become the momentum for me to write columns in the Toronto Joseon Daily for two years. Through these columns, I voiced the world I desired and my thirst for a reasonable human impact that I could contribute. I was satisfied with what I did not have vicariously through these columns. It was a desperate hope for the world I wanted to live in someday.

I intended to share life by writing and to do that, I also needed to read. I had limited time and space to converse with others freely. So, I listened to this world through books. The notion that you can explore the world through books hit home closely, especially then. By flipping through the pages, I met great thoughts, heard beautiful sounds, and saw sceneries that moved my heart. I tried not to relinquish my connection by making time to read and write. I touched the loneliness of my isolated soul. Thus, time spent writing is a time I spent working on myself, and it is time that helped me live. I knocked on my heart with a pen and paper no matter where I was or the time of the day.

Writing also helped me hold on to myself after divorcing my husband. Even when you think that it is better to be apart, the relationship's ending always hurts. Perhaps it is because you mourn the time you spent and the effort you put in to end things, and you grieve the time you spent denying things to put an end to the relationship. I filled the blank page with words and blame that no one would listen to. I did not need to be reasonable and only needed to unleash my feelings since no one was there to object. After I was done pouring my feelings out onto the pages, I would crumple them and then throw them out in the awaiting trash bin. I tried to remove my spiteful heart with the crumpled pages. I do not know for how long I would have lived with spikes in my heart and unbearable pain if I did not write. If I had not had time to calm myself through writing, my emotions may have been much more heightened. My feelings would have built up within me and finally exploded. I would have hurt the ones around me had it not been for my compositions. Writing is my healing time and time to reflect on myself honestly. That is probably why, even today, I walk around with blank pages and pens.

I spent time sharing myself with others. In post-war Korea, when educated talents were the only social asset, the time I spent volunteering for the underprivileged who were excluded from learning opportunities helped me a lot with my inner growth. I felt rewarded through volunteering and sharing, and I realized the happiness of seeing others grow and develop with me. These junctures taught me what a happy life means and made me think honestly about what it means to live like a content human being.

At that time, I also realized that when love becomes the purpose of human life, there is a great sense of happiness. From then on, these values directed my life. The sense of sharing and the pride of volunteering that I felt at that time has led me to where I am needed even now, even after all these years. There are worries around me that I am going through a lot of hard work, but I am not working when volunteering for these people; I am looking for happiness. When I did free acupuncture services for fifteen years after I learned medicine at TCM University, I felt joy and enjoyment through the service. Serving is not just about sharing power, time, or material things but about sharing love. Because of this loving heart, both those who receive help and those who help can be happy. What connects people should be the heart, not anything else. If you do that, you will find that you are receiving much more than you realize. I cannot explain it exactly, but after serving and sharing, my heart always felt lighter and elated.

There are moments when you feel that you are not enough when you share yourself with the world. I was born an explorer. My innate characteristics drive me to try new things, but I have most fun learning something new. Learning about an unknown world helps me realize that I am alive. Learning is the biggest treat I could give myself. It gives me the butterflies and excitement that I could not feel from a charming house and sublime scenery. And because I have those moments, I am who I am today.

Figuring out how beautiful things are in the world is a living dream. The Earth is filled with wonderful places, mesmerizing scenes of nature and incredible people. It is an amazing privilege to be able to explore the world and its inhabitants. It is one of my favourite pass times next to helping others and sharing my time with valuable organizations. You do not have to be a great person or accomplish something big. If you are sincere in your work and enjoy learning, you will feel that something has been formed inside you without realizing it.

You should learn what you want, as long as it is not a bad thing that harms the world. As you learn, you will naturally know whether you are abusing the world. If you like flowers, you can learn about flowers, and if you like cars, you can learn about them. If you do not know what you like, try to start learning about any subject and do not stop until you find something that pulls on your heart.

There are not many things you learn in your life that you start off with the conviction that 'this is it.' I also doubted what I was doing and wondered if I could do it. I wondered what good all my effort was doing. I also had those moments. Still, I believed in the positive power of learning, so I slowed down for a while but never stopped.

All living things begin to learn when they are born. It does not stop until the end of its life. They learn the skills to walk and communicate with the things around them. Since when has learning become exclusively an academic term? Take it from me, learning is not a waste of time. Nor should it be just used for advancement in an occupation or for material success. It should be also done for pleasure. That is when the best learning happens.

All learning is valuable. What we have learned is stored somewhere in our bodies and minds, waiting for the day when it will be useful. All learning is a precious asset that cannot be taken away from anyone and cannot be lost. All learning has made me who I am today and enriched my life. I am grateful for every moment of learning. When I step out to attend my saxophone lesson, my steps are light.

Love Confession…Love is Okay.

I confess my love for the world. I am thankful for every stage of my life and wish to tell myself I did well. I cannot forget the bruises left by the hard and painful times, but I accepted it calmly and acknowledged that it was a part of my life. I am truly grateful that I was able to have the strength, wisdom, and courage to keep myself level-headed amid extreme times. That is why I confess that I still love myself and am full of love for the world. There are many regrets and doubts, but I am very happy that the delightful and rewarding memories remain even deeper.

I started out feeling like I needed to resolve something that was hanging in my heart. I was just going to forget about it and let it go but the nagging discomfort was ever-present, and it could not be ignored. I was about to pass it by, saying that my life was fine as it was. I started off without a clear purpose but then it became a journey for me. It was a path that my daughter's tears led to. It was a selfish desire to heal the wounds in my children's hearts. Today, I am glad I stepped up and reconciled all that was unnerving me deep inside.

My children are the meaning of my life and my pride. They are precious children who have confirmed my faith that God will never leave me alone, even when I am about to give up. I am always grateful that I am blessed to have such beautiful children. I am grateful to God for giving me these children, and I am grateful to my husband. My motivation to take action was that I had to take away the burden that might linger in the hearts of such precious children.

I read an article by a writer once, and he said, "Parents can be the trauma of their children." He calmly unravelled the meaning of reconciliation he felt during his last time with his father, who had been the object of hatred and resentment for a long time. Even before I read the content, I was in a daze, as if I had been hit in the head. Until children become impatient with the thought that if they do not heal the wounds they received from their parents, who are their roots and foundation, they may remain bitter in their hearts. I did. I thought I had to reconcile with the past first so they could have a chance.

I earnestly hope that this unequivocal confession of my life will be a gift to my children and that they can reconcile with the past and cherish their parents as memories instead of burying them deep in their hearts. I tried to tell them the story of my life and how I wanted them to be truly happy. I hope that my earnestness has reached the hearts of my children. And I hope that they will understand me as a human being full of shortcomings but full of love for them.

It took courage. I had changed my mind tens of thousands of times before I started. I cried and laughed a lot at the memories that came to mind while writing. I was grateful for the life I had endured and lived. Someone once said that gratitude is like an alarm clock that wakes up from sleepy happiness. I began to feel at ease when I realized that the moments that were painful for me were the time I needed to grow.

I was also relieved by my feelings of being held back by the world because I thought divorce was the only failure of my life. Human emotions are ever-changing, and no relationship lasts forever. As I look back in time, I admit that I had the arrogance and foolishness to think that I could overcome everything with my patience and sacrifice. But I also realized that the end of a relationship is not a failure. I do not want to be afraid of other people's judgemental eyes and vicious words. I held on to that

DANDELION OF THAT WINTER

fear for a long while even though I did not want to. So, I made no effort to change, I just waited. I also began to reflect on my foolishness. In the first place, it was a mistake to try to find happiness according to someone else's standards.

There are many celibates in the world today. Still, I am an old-fashioned person, so I think it is more fun to get married, have children, and live a good life than to live alone. I believe marriage is a bearable thing to do, and love is something you must do.

I believe that we should not avoid and reject the temptation of an unfamiliar world in advance. Nothing comes without effort, so whatever form of relationship you have with whom you have must be done with zeal. I hope that if you start with love, you will not have to rely only on your uncontrollable heart. If there is a problem, you should try to solve it. Avoiding and bumping into it are not the same. You must face it with all your heart, and if that does not work, you have to muster up the courage to get out of it without regrets. If you have put in all your effort, you do not need to be noticed, just leave quietly and move on without looking back.

There is a need for warmth between people. You cannot tell how warm people are since they do not have measurements like stoves. Therefore, people must express and convey this warmth through words and actions. No relationship can be healthy if you do not communicate. If you think about what happens to stagnant water that cannot flow, you will understand. When you understand the other person and understand yourself through conversation, one another's lives will be enriched. Dialogue is not about one-sidedly conveying one's thoughts or expressing feelings but about giving and receiving feelings to understand each other's feelings and circumstances.

The art of conversation is hard to figure out on its own. I want you to eliminate the arrogance you already know well and hone it through practice and training. There were many moments in my life when I felt how precious it is to have the maturity to express one's love with kind words and a gentle attitude. The saying that the soft triumphs over the strong has often been seen in my life. A warm heart is good to share with many people. It is okay to love a lot.

I want people to be happy. You need to focus on yourself and find happiness within yourself. You cannot live completely without looking at other people's eyes or glances. But do not be a slave to gossip mongering or saving face. It is a waste of valuable time. We should be grateful and content with the reality we are in, and confident to walk proud in our own shoes. But we should never stop dreaming. Do not make the mistake of confusing greed with dreams. As much as we dream and seek those dreams, our lives change. It is not selfish to dream and pursue your dreams. It is something one can do only when they are ready and if you have the fortune to be able to follow your dreams, then you are truly a blessed person.

You should not mistake what others want and yearn for in your dreams. You must ask yourself what you want and find it. If everyone else's dreams sound interesting to you but they do not mean anything to you, I hope you do not fear the world's standards and live the life you want. Even if it is a universal dream that everyone wants, you have to question if that is a dream you wish to pursue.

It is the truth that life is hard to live. A person who has lived through many hardships may have an easier time overcoming them than those who have not. In fact, there is no such thing as a happy life in the first place. Trials and sufferings may always accompany a person's life, like a friend. So, it is a good idea to have a friend who can comfort you whenever you have a hard time. Ultimately, it is most important to be lenient and not swayed by the challenges that life throws you. It is important to have the mindset to be indifferent and to accept it. I want you to keep that positive response close to you and develop the strength to manage your happiness and unhappiness. Remember the saying, "This too shall pass." I have reached the age where I know that there is only a difference in time without having to quote the words of the Bible and that in the end, both joy and sorrow will pass. If misfortune comes, take it easy and control your mind, believing that it will pass someday, and if happiness comes, you can rejoice in it because you do not know when it will pass. In the end, it is up to you. We all experience good times and bad times. For some, there are more of the good times and for others there are more of the bad times. Some of us have very large crosses to bear and others have smaller crosses to bear. Life is not always fair, but it is how we deal with it that counts.

I used to be very upset about being nasty or hated by others. Big and small things piled up, and the psychological damage I suffered from the public commentary was great. The aftermath was long-lasting. I feared that I would hate those who hated me unjustly. I did not want to live my life full of hate because, in the end, we have to live with each other and rely on each other. We cannot live in this world alone. I needed to understand the simple fact that I cannot change other people. Once I recognized that I could not change others, I was able to change myself and change my mindset.

All individuals face unwanted hardships in their life. You can overcome this hardship when you hold your ground and face it alone. I believe that we have to be owners of our own life and guide our lives. You can walk with others and accept the help or consoling only once you can stand for yourself alone. That is life.

Certain passages in books may pull your heartstrings more than other lines. Even in a book, you cannot exactly say that you enjoyed every part of it; there are bound to be some passages that steal your heart. A writer once said that a bookstore is a pharmacy curing your heart, and each book has similar passages to medicine that heals people. With just a couple of words or several sentences, it takes various forms, but it all touches our hearts by offering happiness, love, and respect to our lives. This is why I cannot stop reading and thinking. I hope it is not a big ask that a part of my writing can bring healing moments to my readers.

They tell you not to exercise too much when you are older and to limit your eating—the number of things you can and cannot do increases. There are things you cannot and should not do for too long. But love is okay. You can love a lot. May all the things I love shine in my heart for a long time. I wish they shine like the sunlight radiating through the lush leaves during the day and like the stars bathing the black sky at night. That is why I still love today. Love is okay.

Testimonials...

As a friend of the author and the Korean church in Toronto, Canada, for decades, I was often impressed by how they quietly volunteered in the church kitchen, even if no one recognized them. On the other hand, her prayers deeply touch everyone's souls with immense grace every time she prays that I dare to call the author "Pastor."

I recommend this story of a truly beautiful flower that quietly overcame the difficulties of immigrant life to all those who are looking for hope beyond despair.

-Hon. Raymond Sung Joon Cho, Ministry for Seniors and Accessibility, Ontario

The author's perspective on life's challenges is refreshingly insightful and inspiring. A powerful story that will resonate with so many who have put down roots in Canada and have experienced various challenges often faced by newcomers. A reminder that optimism, hope, and determination will inevitably lead to happiness and success.

-Hon. Michael Parsa, Ministry of Children, Community and Social Services, Ontario

Writing has the power to heal. There is an inner healing power that occurs when you write and a healing energy that resonates with those who read it. The reason why the author has already been able to heal the bodies and minds of many people is because of her dignity as a woman who lived through an era and her soul as a noble 'wounded healer' who willingly shares recovery and growth through the wisdom she has embodied through life.

Through this book, I hope you will have a time of true healing with the author, who turned life's difficulties between Korea and Canada into gold like an alchemist, holding her hand and looking into her eyes.

-Eun Lim, Counsellor

It feels like she is finally out into the world in her colours. The owner of this autobiographical essay, who I did not know had joined the absurdity of married life, held on to the fence of the family with desperate maternal love, protecting the path ahead of her children and leading them to success. For a long time, she had to live a life of injustice driven by the prejudice of society because of unfortunate events in her family. The self-portrait of a woman drawn in this autobiographical essay gets me tearful.

-Jeong Sook Chang, Writer

After reading Park Jeong-ae's collection of works, "Dandelion of That Winter," I feel as if I had encountered an enormous tree. This is the fruit of the artist's sincerity, perseverance, and sincere life. I met Jeong Ae in 1970 as a colleague in the same school. She was a great educator who loved her students with her innate maternal nature.

However, as I listened to the confession of her life, I was shocked. Because I know her personhood, I know how unjust her suffering and suffering are. 'How could this be?' I protested, and I was stunned with sadness and emotion. The essays in "Dandelions of That Winter" are, on the other hand, excellent works. The words that she has to say have been filtered and compressed by themselves over a long period of time, and the use of vocabulary is accurate, even though she has been away from her native tongue for 50 years.

"My mother-in-law came to stay in Canada for a while and witnessed how her son treated me, and said, "You are living well without running away. I didn't give birth to a son like that. If that was my husband, I would have run away more than ten times." and returned to Korea before I gave birth to our youngest."

The mother-in-law's words are more than enough to defend the artist's grief. I would like to pay tribute to her extraordinary perseverance and determination and congratulate her on publishing "Dandelions of that Winter." Now, I hope she will fulfill her desires one by one and enjoy the happiness you delayed with your children who have grown up well.

-Hyang Ah Lee, Poet and a writer

She is a woman of determination who does not fall but rises again like a tumbling doll. Her life was one of learning and challenges, and she overcame it with fortitude. She forgives her relationship with her husband with love, reflects on her marital discord and divorce as her responsibility, and accounts how she must live on for her three children like a confession in her writing.

It is lovely and respectful how the author brilliantly concludes the process of her life with love and aesthetics through her autobiographical essay.

I applaud your courage in challenging and striving through the harsh and winding life given to you in a distant foreign land and even confessing your enlightenment with patience and gratitude. I wish your old age to shine beautifully with your beloved children.

-Jeong Ja Shin, Auditor of Hong ik Hospital

Dandelion of that Winter is a must-read for anyone looking for an inspiring and uplifting story. Jeong Ae Park has crafted a poignant and powerful narrative that will stay with readers long after they turn the last page. This book is not just a story of survival; it is a celebration of the human spirit's determined will to thrive.

One of the most compelling aspects of Dandelion of that Winter is its message of hope and empowerment. Jeong Ae Park's story is a reminder that no matter how insurmountable the obstacles may seem, it is possible to rise above them. Her journey is a beacon of hope for anyone facing similar struggles, showing that with resilience and support, one can overcome even the most daunting challenges.

-Cris Storm, Author

THE END

Map of South Korea showing the cities mentioned in the autobiography.

My colleagues and I and some students
at the YWCA Ahracho Centre.

Family photo from 1984.

Me and two other church members wearing traditional Hanbok dresses.

I was president of the Korean Canadian Women's Association in 1993.

All the reunification members from Canada were invited to the President's house in Seoul, South Korea, in 1997.

Seminar for Comfort Women in Toronto in 1993.

At a camp for the Korean Canadian Physically
Challenged Adult Community in 2015.

Members of the Korean Canadian Physically
Challenged Adult Community in 2016.

My graduation in 2003 from the College of
Traditional Chinese Medicine in Toronto.

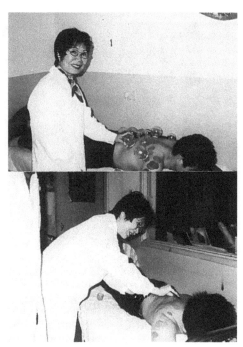

Applying cupping therapy to my patient to relieve
his pain, inflammation and improve blood flow.

Teaching traditional Chinese Medicine at Capital University in Beijing, China in 2004.

Me at the Great Wall of China in 2004.***

About the Author

Jeong Ae (Kim) Park was born in Incheon City, South Korea in 1945. Kim, as she likes to be called now, embarked on a remarkable journey that spanned continents and fields of expertise. Here are her highlights:

Education:

Graduated with a B.Sc. in Biology from Chosun University.
Taught Biology at KeeJeon Girls' High School in the City of Jeonjoo, South Korea.

Worked as a lab assistant in the Department of Biology at the University of Saskatchewan.

Medical and Holistic Practices:

Instructed Chinese traditional medicine at the Canada Chinese Medical University of Toronto Campus (a satellite campus of Beijing Capital University of Medical Science).
Obtained a certificate from the Shiatsu School of Canada.
Completed a degree program in the College of Traditional Chinese Medicine and Pharmacology Canada (affiliated with Beijing Capital University of Medical Science).
Underwent a clinical internship in the Traditional Chinese Medicine Department of Beijing Capital University Hospital.

Community Leadership:

Served as the president of the Korean Canadian Women's Association, the Korean Canadian Literary Association, and the Community of Disabled Adults.
Actively participated as a member of the Peaceful Reunification of the Korean Peninsula, Toronto Chapter.

Current Roles:

Currently serves as an advisor to the Korean Canadian Women's Association.
Holds the position of chair on the Korean Canadian Literary Association Board.
Acts as the general secretary of the Korean Canadian Seniors Music Association.

Recognition and Publications:

Received recognition for 10 years of volunteering from the City of Toronto.

Published works include: *"Dandelion of That Winter," "In the Land I Am Standing On,"* and *"Still the Winter Is Long."*

Kim's dedication to education, medicine, community service, and literature has left an indelible mark on those around her. Her multifaceted contributions continue to inspire and uplift everyone she touches.

www.ingramcontent.com/pod-product-compliance
Lightning Source LLC
Jackson TN
JSHW011717141224
75426JS00001B/2